Criminal Justice
Recent Scholarship

Edited by
Marilyn McShane and Frank P. Williams III

A Series from LFB Scholarly

Urban Politics, Crime Rates, and Police Strength

Thomas D. Stucky

LFB Scholarly Publishing LLC
New York 2005

Copyright © 2005 by LFB Scholarly Publishing LLC

Library of Congress Cataloging-in-Publication Data

Stucky, Thomas Dain
  Urban politics, crime rates, and police strength / Thomas D. Stucky.
      p. cm. -- (Criminal justice)
  Includes bibliographical references and index.
  ISBN 1-59332-090-6 (alk. paper)
  1. Police--United States--Case studies. 2. Crime--United States--
Public opinion. 3. Crime prevention--United States--Finance. 4. Local
government--United States--Citizen participation. 5. Police--
Recruiting--United States--Case studies. 6. Police-community
relations--United States--Case studies. 7. Community policing--United
States--Regional disparities. I. Title. II. Series: Criminal justice (LFB
Scholarly Publishing LLC)
  HV8138.S78 2005
  363.2'0973--dc22

2005004913

ISBN 1-59332-090-6

Printed on acid-free 250-year-life paper.

Manufactured in the United States of America.

Table of Contents

List of Tables and Figures

Acknowledgments

This research was supported by the Center for Research on Crime and Socio-Legal Studies at the University of Iowa. I wish to thank Celesta Albonetti, Robert Baller, Kevin Leicht, and Peverill Squire for their valuable insights and comments on earlier versions of this work. Thanks also to Eric Bleich who provided tremendous research assistance in the production of this book. Most especially, I would like to thank Karen Heimer, whom I admire and respect. I will consider myself fortunate if people think I am half the social scientist she is.

CHAPTER 1:

Introduction

Crime has become one of the most visible areas of public concern in recent years (Maguire and Pastore, 1998: Table 2.1). Yet, crime rates vary tremendously across U.S. cities. For instance, Amherst, New York had 1,940 crimes per 100,000 residents in 2002. Columbia, South Carolina with a similar number of residents had a crime rate of 10,300 for the same year (Maguire and Pastore, 2004: Table 3.110). A number of studies have examined city-level variation in crime rates (for example Bailey, 1984; Lee, 2000; Messner, 1983; Messner and Golden 1992; Miethe, Hughes, and McDowall, 1991; Ousey, 1999; Parker, 2001, 2004; Parker and Johns, 2002; Shihadeh and Flynn, 1996; Shihadeh and Steffensmeier, 1994; Shihadeh and Ousey, 1996; Velez, Krivo, and Peterson, 2003; Wadsworth and Kubrin, 2004). These studies have emphasized a number of social and economic factors such as: poverty, family disruption, ethnic heterogeneity and urbanization, often explicitly or implicitly relying on Shaw and McKay's (1972) social disorganization theory. Until recently, however, these studies have essentially ignored political factors. Recent studies of systemic social disorganization as well as the institutional anomie perspective have begun to suggest that politics and crime are related. Yet, none develop a theory to explain how and why local politics and crime should be related to criminal justice outcomes.

Another major criminal justice research issue is the relationship between crime and formal social control such as police employment, expenditures, and arrests (for example Chamlin and Langworthy, 1996; Jackson, 1989; Jackson and Carroll, 1981; Jacob and Rich, 1981; Jacobs, 1979; Jacobs and Helms, 1997; Jones, 1974; Kent and Jacobs,

1

2004; Levitt, 1997, 2002; Marvell and Moody, 1996; McCrary, 2002; Nalla, Lynch, and Lieber, 1997; Sever, 2001, 2003; Wilson and Boland, 1978). Studies of variation in formal social control have also examined numerous social and economic factors, often based on rational choice, conflict perspectives, and organizational perspectives. Yet, similar to studies of crime, few explicitly consider the role of local politics (for exceptions see Chandler and Gely, 1995; Sever, 2001; Stucky, 2001; Trejo, 1991), and those that do tend not to theorize about the role of local politics, or fail to include all theoretically relevant elements of city political systems. Because political mechanisms are likely shape local anti-crime policies, I argue that research should examine the role that local political actors and systems play in this process. Thus, both studies of crime and formal social control would benefit from greater attention to the role of local institutional politics.

The goal of the current study is to develop a theoretical account of how and why local politics, crime, and formal social control are related. I argue that Hick's and Misra's (1993) *political resource* theory can offer insights into the effect of local politics on crime and crime control in cities. Political resource theory specifies how key state and non-state actors, using the resources available to them as they pursue their perceived interests, shape governmental policy responses. Using insights from political resource theory, I synthesize research from criminal justice studies and studies of state and local politics to develop an *institutional resource* perspective on crime. Then, I apply this logic to study of formal social control to develop an institutional resource perspective on police strength. This institutional resource perspective is used to generate hypotheses about the effect of local political systems and actors on crime rates and police strength in cities. Thus, the goal is to synthesize theory from political sociology and political science with theory in two distinct areas of criminology.

The book is organized as follows: In Chapter 2, I first discuss the most prominent explanation of differences in crime across cities – social disorganization. I next review city-level research on crime, which often uses social disorganization concepts. Then, I discuss some recent theoretical advances in social disorganization theory that highlight the desirability of addressing the relationship between local politics and crime. In the second part of chapter 2, I turn to research which has examined variation in police strength. This research has relied mainly on rational choice, conflict and organizational perspectives. Yet, few studies have examined the effect politics may have on the relative size of police forces. This discussion will show that macro-level theories of crime control can benefit from addressing variation in local politics. Thus, two prominent areas of criminal justice research—variation in crime and police strength across cities—could benefit from exploration into and theorizing about the ways that local politics are likely to matter. In Chapter 3, I argue that political resource theory provides a mechanism for understanding the link between politics, crime, and policing. I, then, review prior research on the impact of local political systems on minority representation, as well as variation in public policy outcomes caused by variation in local political system characteristics. Then, I use insights from this research to develop hypotheses regarding the effects of local politics on crime rates and police strength. Chapter 4 describes the methods and data used to test the hypotheses derived from the institutional resource perspective. Then, in chapter 5, I empirically assess the effect of local politics on variation in crime rates for cities with 25,000 or more residents in both 1980 and 1990. Then, in chapter 6, I test the effect of local political systems on police strength in a similar sample of cities. Finally, in chapter 7, I discuss the implications of the current study for studies of crime and formal control, as well as some directions for future research on the relationships between politics and crime, and politics and policing.

CHAPTER 2:

Extant Research on Crime and Police Strength

A key question in criminology is why cities vary, sometimes dramatically, in their rates of crime. City-level studies of crime have examined numerous social and economic factors such as: poverty, urbanization, race, family disruption, and disadvantage. Although not always explicitly stated, many city-level explanations of crime rely on social disorganization theory (Miethe et al., 1991). In the first part of this chapter, I discuss social disorganization theory and city-level research that has examined social disorganization concepts. Then, I examine some recent advances in social disorganization theory that highlight the importance of examining the role of local politics, as well as some recent research which has begun to consider the relationship between politics and crime. Following that I discuss research on another key question in criminology—why cities vary in formal social control. In Part II of this chapter I discuss extant research on variation on formal social control at the city-level. This discussion will highlight the most prominent explanations that have been used previously – rational choice, conflict, and organizational perspectives—and show that none have paid much theoretical attention to local politics. Therefore, the goal of this chapter is to show that two key issues in criminology – city-level variation in crime and crime control – can benefit from theoretical attention to the effects of local politics.

5

EXPLAINING CITY CRIME RATES

One of the earliest sociological explanations of group-level variation in crime is social disorganization theory (Shaw and McKay, 1972). Social disorganization refers to the inability of the community to realize common values or solve collective problems (Bursik, 1988). Social disorganization theory posits that crime rates in a community are related to the level of community organization. It assumes that there is general agreement over norms for behavior among community members, and that crime rates increase when communities are unable to organize to enforce these norms. In Shaw and McKay's (1972) original formulation, *socio-economic status, ethnic heterogeneity,* and *residential mobility* are all posited to inhibit the development of social ties among community residents, which limits the ability of the community to maintain social control (for discussions see Bursik, 1988; Bursik and Grasmick, 1993).

More recently, researchers have suggested that *urbanization* and *family disruption* are also important determinants of community organization (for example Sampson, 1987; Sampson and Groves, 1989). For instance, Sampson and Groves (1989), use the 1982 and 1984 British Crime Survey (10,905 residents in 238 communities across Great Britain) to test the intervening mechanisms of informal social control that the theory posits. They include measures of sparse friendship networks, unsupervised teen groups, and low organizational participation as indicators of lack of informal social control. They find that the intervening variables account for most of effect of structural variables such as poverty and family disruption on crime. Recently, Lowenkamp, Cullen, and Pratt (2003) replicate Sampson and Groves' classic study using 1994 BSC data. The authors generally find strong support for the social disorganization model as elaborated by Sampson and Groves and in the 7 of 23 cases where coefficients significantly differ between the 1982 and 1994 BCS samples, all are more favorable to social disorganization theory than the original study. Therefore, the authors suggest that the social disorganization model is strongly supported. In the next section, I review research that examines social disorganization concepts in city-level crime research.

Poverty

Consistent with the social disorganization perspective, poverty has long been considered an important factor in predicting city-level variation in crime rates (Bailey, 1984; Liska, Logan, and Bellair, 1998; Loftin and Parker, 1985; Parker, 2004; Peterson and Krivo, 1993; Sampson, 1985; Shihadeh and Ousey, 1996; Wadsworth and Kubrin, 2004; Williams, 1984). Theoretically, communities with greater poverty are thought to lack resources necessary for community organization and supervision of youth (Sampson and Groves 1989). Despite strong theoretical reasons to expect a relationship between poverty and crime, empirical support has been mixed. For instance, Bailey (1984) and Williams (1984) find support for a poverty-crime relationship, whereas others have suggested that income inequality is a more important determinant of crime (for example Blau and Blau, 1982; Messner, 1982). Land, McCall and Cohen (1990) suggest that one reason for the mixed findings in prior research on poverty and inequality is the difficulty of identifying independent effects of each because cities with high concentrations of poverty are also likely to have high levels of income inequality.

Some recent studies look not at poverty per se but aspects of the labor market which produce unemployment, poverty and inequality. For instance, Parker (2004) examines the link between race/ gender specific labor market outcomes, particularly as the result of economic restructuring from an industrial to a service economy and race/ gender specific homicide rates from 1980 to 1990, and uses a time series strategy to capture the dynamic shift in labor markets from industrial to service based economies over time. She suggests that restructuring from and industrial to a service economy produces social disorganization which leads to homicide. The sample includes 168 cities with 100,000 or more residents in 1980 and 1990. She uses the Supplementary Homicide Reports as the source for homicide data (five-year averages) and includes race and gender specific measures of poverty, inequality, segregation, and percent of households receiving assistance, as well as percent black and percent Hispanic. Using negative binomial and poisson pooled cross sectional time series data, Parker (2004) finds that economic restructuring had a disproportionate impact on black homicide offending and seemed to benefit whites. She also finds that disadvantage appeared to be associated with homicide for blacks only. She also finds that police presence reduced homicides in three of the four groups. Thus, differences in economic experiences by race and gender, particularly in terms of the kinds of labor market each group faces affected homicide rates for each group. In sum, the accumulated weight of the evidence suggests that economic disadvantage is an important predictor of city-level variation in crime.

Urbanization

Another factor suggested by the social disorganization approach and extensively examined in previous city-level research is urbanization. Sampson and Groves (1989) suggest that larger city populations have a decreased capacity for informal social control. Urbanization is thought to weaken local friendship ties, increase anonymity, and impede participation in local affairs, forcing larger cities to rely more heavily on formal social control mechanisms of the state. City-level studies of crime have generally operationalized this concept by including a measure of the size of the city population (for example Liska et al., 1998; Messner and Golden, 1992; Parker and McCall, 1999; Peterson and Krivo, 1993; Shihadeh and Steffensmeier, 1994). Previous studies consistently find that as population size increases crime increases (for a review see Land et al., 1990). In a recent study, Nolan (2004) confirms the relationship between population size and crime in a study of 1294 cities with 25,000 or more residents in 1990 (similar to the universe of cities used in the current study). Across all cities in the sample, there was a small but significant positive correlation between crime rate and population size.[1] Thus, the weight of the research suggests that urbanization and crime are positively related, consistent with social disorganization theory.

Family Disruption

Another factor thought to be an important determinant of community organization is family disruption. Sampson (1987) suggests three reasons family disruption may be related to crime. The first is the traditional view that broken homes are related to delinquency because non-intact families have less control over their own children. Second, informal social control at the neighborhood level is expected to be lower in single parent families because single parents have less time to monitor neighborhood children. Finally, non-intact families are associated with lower community-level informal social control because participation by single parents in local community activities, such as the PTA, is low. Numerous studies have found support for the relationship between family disruption and city-level variation in crime (for example Liska et al., 1998; Messner and Golden, 1992; Peterson and Krivo, 1993; Sampson, 1987; Shihadeh and Flynn, 1996; Shihadeh and Steffensmeier, 1994).

Recent studies have also begun to suggest that the notion of the two-parent biological family may be dated and require more nuanced thinking about what aspects of family relationships/ breakdowns should be expected to be related to crime. For instance, Parker and Johns (2002) examine the link between family structure, family disruption, and race specific homicide for 144 large cities in 1990. They distinguish between diversity in family structure and family disruption. Family disruption refers to a breakup of a family unit through divorce whereas family diversification refers to a surrogate family unit. They argue that the structural conditions that urban blacks face means that many have developed alternative family structures. The authors find that family disruption is primarily a factor in white homicides but not black homicide rates. In another study, Rebellon (2002) reviews the broken homes-crime relationship, and argues that there are several possible reasons for such a link. It could be that the loss of a parent weakens social control. Or it could be that the reason for the broken home is marital conflict. Research seems to support the latter to a certain extent. He argues that the failure to distinguish between reasons for and types of broken homes has reduced the likelihood of finding a broken homes-delinquency link the past. The author finds a link between different types of broken homes and status, property and violent offenses using the National Youth Survey. Single parent families per se do not seem to increase delinquency at the individual level. It appears that parental conflict may be more related to crime since recent remarriage also increased the likelihood of delinquency.

Thus, family disruption seems to be related to crime, but it is not the breakup per se but the conflict that led to the breakup that is the underlying cause. Rebellon (2002) also suggests that community-level studies which show crime higher in areas with higher rates of female headed households could reflect the inability to monitor *other* people's kids, consistent with social disorganization theory and Sampson (1987).

Ethnic Heterogeneity

Shaw and Mckay (1972) hypothesized that ethnic heterogeneity inhibited the development of community ties among residents. If people come from different racial and ethnic backgrounds, they are less likely to interact, particularly if there are significant language barriers to overcome (as in the city of Chicago at the time of their writing). Although the original formulation of social disorganization focused on people of different national origins, more recent research has considered primarily racial and ethnic differences of Americans. Thus, much research has focused on the race-crime relationship (Liska and Bellair, 1995; Liska et al., 1998; Parker and McCall, 1999; Peterson and Krivo, 1993; Sampson, 1985; Shihadeh and Flynn, 1996; Shihadeh and Ousey, 1996; Shihadeh and Steffensmeier, 1994). Early studies often focused on a black subculture of violence (for example Messner, 1983; Sampson, 1985, 1987) or the effects of differences in poverty or income inequality across race (see Blau and Blau, 1982; Messner and Golden, 1992). Current debate on the race-crime relationship centers on the very different social structural situations facing most African-Americans.

For instance, Sampson (1987) argues that much of the race-crime relationship can be accounted for by the link between black unemployment, family disruption and crime. Following research by social demographers, he argues that high rates of black male unemployment limit the desirability of black men as marriage partners. As a consequence, blacks and whites have very different patterns of marriage and ultimately family structure. In an analysis of 150 cities in 1980, Sampson (1987) finds that black robbery and homicide rates are related to family disruption, even controlling for income, region, age composition, density, city size, and welfare benefits. He also finds that the effects of family disruption are similar for whites and blacks. Sampson finds that the error terms between the black and white equations are positively correlated, suggesting that factors not included in the model are positively related. This mitigates against the notion that the causes of black crime are rooted in unique aspects of black culture. Thus, he concludes that family disruption is an important determinant of black-white differences in violent crime, and largely mediates the link between unemployment and crime among blacks.

More recently, Shihadeh and Shrum (2004) argue that one of the most consistent findings is the link between race and serious crime. The problem is that theories typically do not ascribe any causal priority to race. Most suggest, as Sampson (1987) does, that neighborhood social structure rather than race is the cause of differences in crime. Yet, few studies have been done at the neighborhood-level to see if the race-crime relationship is truly accounted for by social structure. The authors examine 276 block groups in Baton Rouge, Louisiana, which is their proxy for neighborhoods. Shihadeh and Shrum (2004) examine official statistics on both property and violent offenses, and include block group level indicators of population size, population density, percent age 15-24, female-headed households, poverty, unemployment, income inequality, vacant households, and recent movers. They find that the structural factors that they include completely explain the race-crime relationship and suggest that invoking cultural factors is premature at this point since their results suggest that it is deprivation rather than race that leads to crime.

Disadvantage

Consistent with this, recently a number of scholars have argued that differences in crime rates are the result of large differences in structural and cultural contexts across communities (for example Krivo and Peterson, 1996, 2000; Parker and McCall, 1999). This combination of factors has been termed "disadvantage". The concept of disadvantage is in many ways similar to that of social disorganization, referring to a combination of factors including unemployment, poverty, family disruption, and social isolation.

Sampson and Wilson (1995) argue that high levels of violent crime by African-Americans are the result of the concentration of poverty and family disruption in the black inner city. They note that poor blacks tend to live in poor neighborhoods while poor whites tend to live in non-poor neighborhoods. Following Wilson (1987), they suggest that de-industrialization, and the resulting structural unemployment and exodus of middle and upper-income blacks left extremely poor inner city neighborhoods where only poor blacks live. In addition to the structural problems of high unemployment and poverty, many blacks also face cultural social isolation from mainstream society because opportunities for contact outside one's neighborhood are very limited. Thus, Sampson and Wilson (1995) suggest that black-white differences in crime are the result of the very different neighborhood contexts in which African Americans and whites find themselves.

Krivo and Peterson (1996) also draw on Wilson's (1987) work to argue that blacks and whites find themselves in very different structural circumstances. They suggest that extremely high poverty is associated with very high levels of crime because kids have few positive role models, few jobs are available, few resources are available for social control, and there is a high degree of isolation from mainstream society. Although Krivo and Peterson (1996) suggest a race-invariant model, they note that extremely disadvantaged white neighborhoods are much less common than extremely disadvantaged black neighborhoods, resulting in much higher crime rates for blacks than whites. They test the arguments using 1990 census tract data from Columbus, Ohio. They find that extreme disadvantage (40% or more in poverty) is associated with very high levels of violent crime for both whites and blacks, but blacks have a much higher violent crime rate because they are much more likely to live in these extremely disadvantaged neighborhoods. Parker and McCall (1999) also suggest that the very different social structural situations of blacks and whites explain variation in inter and intra-racial homicide patterns.

Another recent paper examines by Velez, Krivo, and Peterson (2003) examines the gap in black white homicide offending as a function of black-white gaps in disadvantage as well as resources. They suggest that recent research shows that blacks and whites live in very different conditions and some research suggests that different factors may affect offending but these different conditions exist within the same city. Therefore, the *gap* in offending is important to explain as well. Velez and her colleagues (2003) argue that disadvantage and resources may not be opposite ends of the same spectrum. They suggest that disadvantage may promote risk for homicide whereas resources may promote protection from homicide risk. They study the black-white gap in homicide in 126 cities with 100,000 residents and at least 5,000 blacks in 1990 as a function of gaps in young males, homeownership, poverty, female-headed households, male joblessness, income, college education, and number of professionals, controlling for population size, region, segregation and percent black. They note that black white gaps in disadvantage and resources vary considerably from city to city. They find that gaps in segregation and gaps in homeownership increase the black-white gap in homicide, whereas their measures of disadvantage have no impact, but resource measures (W-B gap in: income, college graduates, and number of professionals) increase the homicide gap. Thus, as whites have more resources relative to blacks the black-white homicide gap gets bigger. Velez and her colleagues (2003) argue that their results are consistent with social disorganization theory, which suggests that resources allow an area to protect itself against crime. They suggest that part of this is due to increased political efficacy of areas with high resources, which foreshadows the issues to be considered below. Thus, differences in resources across communities seem to account for differences in homicide by race. The weight of the evidence suggests that differences in resources across neighborhoods account for much of the differences in crime.

In sum, social disorganization concepts have enjoyed empirical support in criminological research. Research suggests that social disorganization concepts – such as poverty, urbanization, ethnic heterogeneity, family disruption, and disadvantage – are associated with high rates of crime. Thus, empirically social disorganization seems to be a viable explanation for variation in crime across cities.

Social disorganization research continues along several lines. For instance, one line of research examines the link between social ties and crime (for example Bellair, 1997; Sampson, 1988; Warner, 2003; Warner and Rountree, 1997). In a recent article, Warner (2003) links disadvantage and social ties to develop what she terms "cultural disorganization". She argues that disadvantage leads to weakened social ties and weak social ties limit the ability to articulate widely held norms. Thus, weakened social ties cause people to perceive others as less likely to hold conventional values (attenuated culture), and as consequence informal social control is weakened and crime goes up. Other research examines smaller units of analysis, such as neighborhoods, and face-blocks (for example Smith, Frazee, and Davison, 2000; Taylor, 1997; Warner and Pierce, 1993), or social disorganization in non-metropolitan contexts (for example Osgood and Chambers, 2000). In the next section, I discuss another recent theoretical development in systemic social disorganization research— collective efficacy.

Collective Efficacy

A significant recent development in the systemic social disorganization tradition is Sampson and his colleague's work on collective efficacy (Morenoff, Sampson, and Raudenbush, 2001; Sampson and Raudenbush, 1997, 1999; Sampson, Morenoff, and Earls, 1999). Collective efficacy refers to social cohesion of neighbors combined with a willingness to intervene on behalf of the common good (Sampson and Raudenbush, 1997). Sampson and his colleagues argue that collective efficacy explains why some areas are more able to maintain informal social control than others. Several recent studies have suggested the utility of collective efficacy as a means of reducing crime.

For example, Sampson and Raudenbush (1997) examine the relationship between collective efficacy and violence in a multi-level study of 343 Chicago neighborhoods, which combines a 1995 residential survey of 8782 residents with homicide and census data. The authors argue that collective efficacy mediates the relationship between individual and neighborhood social demographic characteristics and violent crime. They use three indicators of violence: perceived neighborhood violence, personal victimization and homicide statistics. They find that the effects of residential mobility, concentrated disadvantage, and immigration on violence are somewhat or fully mediated by collective efficacy. Concentrated disadvantage and immigration are negatively associated with collective efficacy whereas residential stability is positively associated with collective efficacy. The authors also find that the association between collective efficacy and violence remained even when controlling for friendship ties and organizational participation.

Another study by Sampson and Raudenbush (1999) examines the broken windows thesis that evidence of minor disorder leads to more serious crime. Employing a unique research technique, the authors use systematic observations of physical and social disorder in Chicago streets to examine the broken windows thesis. They argue that the relationship between disorder and more serious crime is actually spurious once collective efficacy is controlled. They suggest that evidence of disorder is actually just the other end of the crime seriousness spectrum since most evidence of disorder is actually evidence of minor crimes. Thus, they argue that the direct effect of broken windows on crime is minimal. They suggest that the effect may actually be indirect since evidence of disorder actually could causes changes in land use patterns and declines in property values which would in turn lead to loss of collective efficacy and eventually greater crime. Another study by Morenoff et al., (2001) examines the link between collective efficacy and homicide. The study includes two different indicators of homicide-police incident data 1996-98 and vital statistics data for 1996. The study also considers spatial effects and both concentrated disadvantage and concentrated affluence. They find that collective efficacy is a strong predictor of homicide, regardless of the measure, even controlling for prior homicides. Finally, Reisig and Cancino (2004) examine the collective efficacy model using hierarchical linear poisson models in non-metropolitan communities. They find that the collective efficacy model explains crime in non-metropolitan areas as well. Thus, recent research suggests that collective efficacy is an important determinant of crime rates, which is consistent with the focus on informal social control in prior social disorganization research.

Despite these theoretical and methodological advancements, Bursik (1988) and Kubrin and Weitzer (2003) note that one long-standing critique of social disorganization theory is its nearly exclusive focus on *internal* community dynamics. Bursik and Grasmick (1993) suggest that Shaw and McKay (1972) assumed that the ecological factors affecting community development and social mobility patterns were natural processes. Therefore, the external context surrounding a community had little to do with processes internal to the community. Bursik (1988) argues that this is a significant shortcoming, because community development patterns are greatly affected by local governmental decisions. Similarly, Kubrin and Weitzer (2003) argue that social disorganization theory needs to consider external influences on communities such as politics and policing. In the next section I discuss some recent advances in social disorganization theory that begin to address the role of processes external to the community-namely politics.

Public Control and Crime

Recognizing the limitations of extant social disorganization theory, Bursik and Grasmick (1993) begin to address the relationship between the neighborhood and its surrounding context. Based on Hunter (1985), they posit that there are three levels of control that are important for determining the ability of the community to organize against crime. The *private* level involves informal social control of family and close friends. The *parochial* level concerns informal social control that occurs naturally within communities as people interact in their daily routines. Finally, *public* control involves the relationship between the community and outside elements of social control such as the police and other government agencies. There are many situations in which communities may attempt to influence public decision-making. For example, Bursik and Grasmick (1993:53-55) suggest that governmental decisions regarding zoning and land-use more generally are likely to affect who is willing to move into or stay in particular neighborhoods, and therefore, will have important consequences for residential stability and the ability of residents to maintain property values. Thus, it makes sense to consider the relationship between the neighborhood and the city government in determining the ability of the community to organize itself against crime.

Recent social disorganization research has begun to focus on the role that public control plays in inhibiting crime. For instance, Peterson, Krivo, and Harris (2000) study how variation in local institutions affects violent crime rates in neighborhoods in Columbus, Ohio. They argue that neighborhood institutions affect the link between disadvantage and violent crime. Libraries and recreation centers reduce crime by structuring time and providing opportunities for interaction among community residents, which enhance social control. On the other hand, bars increase opportunities for crime and victimization. They find that areas with bars have higher violence, not surprisingly. Recreation centers, on the other hand, inhibit violent crime – but only in areas with high levels of disadvantage. They suggest that communities can enhance public control by increasing their institutional base and fighting the introduction of disorganizing influences such as bars.

In another examination of public control and crime, McNulty and Holloway (2000) focus on public housing projects. They suggest that the race-crime link found in previous literature may be partly explained by the way housing projects anchor disadvantage and create crime-prone areas. In Atlanta, they find that the proximity to local public housing projects explains much of the race-violent crime relationship across 1990 census blocks. Similarly, Bursik (1989) argues that in the 1970s public housing projects in Chicago were placed in neighborhoods that were unable to muster the political clout to block construction. This research suggests that public housing and crime are related and that the placement of these projects depends on the interaction of neighborhoods with the local government. In another recent study, Velez (2001) examines the relationship between disadvantage, public control and victimization in 60 neighborhoods across three cities. She finds that the risk of victimization is lower where public control is higher but this effect appeared to vary by neighborhood context. Specifically, increases in public control had the greatest effect on personal victimizations in the most disadvantaged neighborhoods.

Similarly, Silver and Miller (2004) consider levels of control. They note that the social disorganization literature points to informal social control as the reason for high crime in disorganized neighborhoods but few studies have examined the sources of informal social control. They examine whether social ties, neighborhood attachment and satisfaction with police lead to greater control, and to what extent these factors mediate the link between disadvantage and informal control. They use hierarchical linear models (HLM) on neighborhoods in the city of Chicago. They find that 75% of the variation across neighborhoods in informal social control is due to neighborhood effects rather than the individuals that live there. After controlling for individual level-factors and disadvantage, the authors find that neighborhood attachment and satisfaction with the police are significant predictors of informal social control. Silver and Miller (2004) suggest that satisfaction with the police is higher when police are responsive to the needs of the community. The authors also point to Velez and suggest that private and parochial controls are stronger when partnered with public institutions. Thus, it appears that parochial and public controls may be interrelated.

Rose and Clear (1998) also suggest that, although it is tempting to think of levels of community control as distinct, they are, in reality, interdependent. They suggest that parochial controls are far more likely to be effective in the context of strong private controls. Public controls also interact with parochial private controls, according to Rose and Clear (1998). Rose and Clear (1998) also suggest that the political organization of a community may be a critical factor in community organization against crime. They point to the existence of well-developed internal *political and social institutions* as key factors affecting the ability of the community to address problems that arise. They also suggest that participation in local political activities is determined in part by the belief in their efficacy. Thus, local political participation is more likely to the extent that community residents believe that it will produce desired results.

Triplett, Gainey, and Sun (2003) also focus on the role of institutions in the social disorganization model. They suggest that the strength of neighborhood institutions will be related to all three levels of control and to neighborhood crime rates. Similarly, Sun, Triplett, and Gainey (2004) suggest that formal and informal social control are related and that the strength of institutions is important for informal social control. In particular they examine trust in local government and satisfaction with police in Indianapolis and St. Petersburg, Florida. They predict that neighborhood institutional strength will affect the legitimacy of public institutions—the police and the local government—and this will affect neighborhood crime rates. Sun et al. (2004) find that neighborhoods with higher rates of perceived legitimacy of local government have greater levels of trust and coordinated action among residents, which in turn are associated with lower robbery and burglary rates.

The recognition that social control operates at more than one level, and that these levels interact, represents an important theoretical advancement in social disorganization theory. Yet, because the mechanisms by which various levels of control affect crime, especially public control are only beginning to be addressed, research has not considered whether variation in the city's political context might influence public control.

> However, if public control is about the relationship between neighborhoods and the city government, then examining the *internal* determinants of neighborhood organization only addresses half the relationship. The *external* political environment is also likely to affect the ability of neighborhoods to develop the ties with local government necessary to increase public control and reduce crime (Stucky, 2003: 1103).

Because the political context surrounding a neighborhood varies across cities, it seems worthwhile to consider how that variation may affect government response to community attempts to secure resources. In the next section, I briefly discuss criminological research which has begun to consider the relationship between politics and crime.

POLITICS AND CRIME

In one of the earliest studies of politics and variation in crime across cities, Shihadeh and Flynn (1996) argue that the political strength of various groups will be related to crime. They argue that segregation, politics, and crime are related. "Black isolation from whites may also lead to political ... disenfranchisement of black neighborhoods (Shihadeh and Flynn, 1996: 1332)." They argue that black social isolation may reduce the likelihood that neighborhoods will be able to procure services from the city government (i.e. maintain public control), which will reduce the community' ability to fight crime. One political resource that communities may have is representation on city councils. They study segregation, politics and black crime rates in 150 large cities in 1990. They include the proportion of city council members that are black divided by the proportion of city's voting age population that is black as an indicator of black empowerment. Values below one suggest that the black community is politically underrepresented and values equal to or greater than one suggest that the black community is politically empowered. Shihadeh and Flynn (1996) did not find that their measure of black political empowerment was consistently related to black violence but there may be several reasons why this is the case. First, they only included one element of local politics. In the next chapter, I discuss several other elements of politics that may be relevant. Second, they studied a relatively small number of large cities. It may be that including a larger number of cities would increase the variation in politics and make it more likely to find relationships with crime. Still, their study is the first that I am aware of to include direct measures of city politics in a model of crime rates.

Other studies have also begun to include elements of politics. For instance, Jacobs and O'Brien (1998) find cities with African-American mayors have fewer police killings of citizens. Similarly, Jacobs and Carmichael (2002) find that homicides and assaults on police officers occur less often in cities with African-American mayors. They suggest that this is due to higher levels of political efficacy among blacks in cities where they are descriptively represented in the mayor's office. Finally, Jacobs and Wood (1999) find that African American mayors influence levels of interracial homicides, although Wadsworth and Kubrin (2004) did not find a similar effect in their study of black inter- and intra-racial homicides. Still, the evidence seems to suggest that aspects of local politics are related to crime rates. Thus, further research seems warranted.

Research has also examined other elements of politics and crime. For instance Rosenfeld, Messner, and Baumer (2001) studied the link between social capital and homicide. They suggest that social capital is likely to reduce homicide. One element of social capital is civic engagement. "... High levels of civic engagement should strengthen social organization, and promote informal social control, thereby yielding lower levels of crime and violence (Rosenfeld et al., 2001: 286)." Therefore, communities with higher levels of civic engagement should be more likely to gain external resources such as policing and thereby reduce crime. Their measure of civic engagement is the proportion of the eligible population that voted. Yet, political participation has been shown to be variation in local political systems. In particular, non-partisan voting systems have been shown to depress voter turnout (Alford and Lee, 1968; Hajnal and Lewis, 2003; Karnig and Walter, 1977, 1983). Thus, one element of social capital, civic engagement, could be affected by the structure of city political systems. In a state-level test of institutional anomie theory, Chamlin and Cochran (1995), found that voter turnout mediated the link between poverty and property crime. As voter turnout increased, the link between poverty and property crime declined.

Similarly, institutional anomie theory considers the relationship between politics and crime. This theory suggests that the dominance of economic institutions over non-economic institutions (schools, churches, and the polity) accounts for America's high crime rate (Messner and Rosenfeld, 1997a). Testing this notion, Messner and Rosenfeld (1997b), in a cross-national study of homicide rates find that homicide is lower in countries where the government protects citizens from market forces through welfare programs. In a similar study, Savolainen (2000) finds that homicide and inequality are related but that the strength of the relationship depends on the quality of the country's welfare program. Thus, as welfare program quality increases, the inequality-homicide link decreases. Similarly, Pratt and Godsey (2003), in a cross-national analysis of homicide as a function of social support find that social support (percent of Gross Domestic Product to health care) reduces homicide. Hannon and DeFronzo (1998) found similar results for the relationship between public assistance and crime rates for 406 large metropolitan counties. They find that resource deprivation has significantly less impact on crime rates in areas with higher levels of welfare assistance. Finally, in a county-level analysis of institutional anomie theory, Maume and Lee (2003) examine the relationship between economics, non-economic factors and homicide, including measures of voter turnout, as well as education and welfare expenditures. They find that non-economic institutions directly and substantially reduce the impact of inequality on homicide, as well as consistent negative effects of voter turnout on homicide.

These recent studies suggest empirical support for the relationship between politics and crime. Yet, none address the possibility that there could be systematic differences across cities in the ability of citizens to affect the political process, which may affect the ability to garner resources to maintain informal social control and reduce crime. Political science research, discussed in Chapter 3, suggests that variation in local political systems can affect the ability of the poor and minorities to gain political representation and affects public policy outcomes. I argue that this variation in local political systems across cities will also affect the ability of communities to organize against crime. Indeed, Stucky (2003) finds that certain types of city political systems are associated with lower violent crime rates in cities with 25,000 or more residents in 1990. Thus, it appears that further theorizing on the relationship between city politics and crime is warranted. In the next section, I review another major criminal justice research area – formal social control. This discussion will highlight some important ways in which the study of formal social control would also benefit from the consideration of local politics.

EXTANT RESEARCH ON POLICE STRENGTH

As noted earlier, numerous studies examine the relationship between crime and social control by the state (for example Eitle, D'Alessio, and Stolzenberg, 2002; Jackson and Carroll, 1981; Jackson, 1986, 1989; Jacobs, 1979; Jacobs and Helms, 1997; Kent and Jacobs, 2004; Levitt, 1997; Marvell And Moody, 1996; Mccrary, 2002; Nalla, Lynch, And Lieber, 1997; Sever, 2001, 2003; Stolzenberg, D'alessio, And Eitle. 2004; Wilson And Boland, 1978). These studies have focused on many different conceptions of state social control such as police employment or expenditures, variation in arrests, and styles of policing, just to name a few. I focus on variation in the size of the police force here because it is perhaps the most visible manifestation of formal social control and when citizens call for changes in policing in response to crime the most common demand is for more police.[2] Studies of city-level variation in police strength have often been motivated by the differing predictions of rational choice and conflict theories, as well as organizational theories. Although studies have generally found some support for each perspective, I argue that all three would benefit from consideration of the effects of local politics on formal social control.

Rational Choice

The rational choice perspective assumes that allocation of resources to policing generally will respond to changes in the level of crime. Rational choice theories typically posit that variation in crime is related to the actions of various criminal justice agencies. Whether in the form of increased penalties for convictions, or increased likelihood of arrest, rational choice theory posits that the incidence of crime in a city will be related to the relationship between potential consequences of unlawful activity and potential gains. By implication, increases in the number of police on the street should reduce crime by increasing the likelihood of negative consequences for offenders. Thus, from a rational choice perspective one would expect that increases in crime would lead to increases in police employment, which would subsequently reduce crime.

Rational choice theories also generally assume that local anti-crime policies are produced through a rational aggregation of individual interests in the form of voting (Loftin and McDowall, 1982). Increases in crime lead to greater voter concern, resulting in pressure for action from the local government. Local governments are assumed to respond in the general public interest by increasing the number of police on the street. Of course, the responses of city government are constrained by the availability of resources. Cities must make decisions regarding the way limited revenues are allocated. To the extent that cities have more monetary resources available they will be better able to address numerous priorities. Thus, ceteris paribus, cities with more resources will be more likely to devote more resources to crime control. Consequently, many have included measures of overall city revenues, as a constraint on crime control (for example Jackson and Carroll, 1981; Greenberg et al., 1985; Jackson, 1986, 1989; McDowall and Loftin, 1986; Chamlin, 1989, 1990). Yet, these studies have mainly included fiscal capacity as a control variable with little substantive import. As discussed in Chapter 3, fiscal capacity is a theoretically important variable in political resource theory.

Although the implications of rational choice models are relatively clear, there has been limited empirical support for the notion that local changes in police employment occur directly in response to changes in the crime rate (Greenberg and Kessler, 1982; Loftin and McDowall, 1982). Indeed, some studies have actually found that increases in police activity were associated with increases in reported crime rates (see Levitt, 1998 for a review).

Conflict Theories

A major alternative to rational choice theories of policing comes from the conflict perspective. Conflict theories usually highlight the role of economic conflict (for example Chambliss and Seidman, 1982; Piven and Cloward, 1971; Quinney, 1977; Turk, 1969), or racial/ ethnic conflict (for example Blalock, 1967) in generating state social control. Despite a number of important differences between these approaches, each assumes that resources in society are limited, groups compete for these limited resources and power among groups is unequal. Since limited resources cannot provide for everyone, certain groups use their power to garner benefits for themselves to the detriment of others.

Economic Conflict
One prominent strand of conflict theories of policing comes from Neo-Marxist theories. This approach generally assumes that formal social control efforts will be directed toward protecting the interests of the economically powerful, who have greater access to and control over the state. Thus, from the Neo-Marxist perspective, the size of the police force is expected to be related to unemployment, poverty and/ or

inequality, which threaten the interests of economic elites (Liska, Lawrence, and Benson, 1981). Therefore, police strength is expected not to vary with crime rates per se but with the perceived threat to moneyed interests from economically marginalized groups. Research has generally found some support for the role of economic conflict in accounting for variation in crime control, particularly in comparison to rational choice theories (Greenberg, Kessler, and Logan, 1979; Liska, et al., 1981; Liska, Chamlin, and Reed, 1985).

Although not generally discussed in this literature, many of the propositions suggested by conflict theories are consistent with Black's (1976) theory of law. Black argues that governmental social control is a function of social stratification, and social and cultural distance. As stratification and social and cultural distance increase, Black predicts the amount of law will increase. Thus, at the city-level, one might expect to find that as income inequality increases there will be more police. Recent cross-national research also confirms the relationship economic inequality and police strength. Kent and Jacobs (2004), in a study of 11 nations from 1975 to 1994, find that economic inequality and crime (in more recent years) are related to police strength. Interestingly, minority presence is associated with police strength only in the United States.

One debate within the economic conflict approach is the theoretical and empirical importance of absolute versus relative deprivation (poverty versus inequality). Some would argue that absolute deprivation leads to a greater temptation to engage in instrumental crimes to gain access to goods that would not otherwise be available. Others suggest that inequality leads to frustration on the part of non-elites as they compare themselves to economic elites. Land, et al., (1990) suggest that from a practical standpoint it may be very difficult to tease out these relationships because areas with high poverty also tend to have high levels of income inequality. Despite disagreement over the relative explanatory importance of absolute versus relative deprivation (for example Greenberg, et al., 1985; Jackson 1986; Jackson and Carroll, 1981; Jacobs, 1979; Liska and Chamlin, 1984) overall empirical support for the economic conflict approach is fairly consistent in prior research.

Racial/ Ethnic Threat

A second strand of crime control research from a conflict perspective focuses on the perceived threat of ethnic or racial minorities. Blalock (1967) suggests that racial/ ethnic competition generate conflict. Unlike Neo-Marxist theories for which competition is between economic classes, for these theorists the primary competition for resources is between various racial/ ethnic groups. Thus, although the mechanism is similar to Neo-Marxist theories, crime control will vary according to the perceived threat posed by the presence of ethnic/ racial minorities rather than the threat from the economically marginalized. Consistent with this, Liska, Lawrence, and Sanchirico (1982) find that the presence of nonwhites is related to fear of crime in cities for both whites and nonwhites, irrespective of variation in crime. This suggests that citizen pressure for increases in police employment might be generated by the presence of minorities even in the absence of changes in crime rates. As noted in Sever's (2003) extensive literature review on the topic, numerous studies find that the presence of racial and ethnic minorities is related to increases in crime control (for example Chamlin, 1989; Jackson, 1986, 1989; Liska, et al., 1981; Liska and Chamlin, 1984; Liska, et al., 1985, but compare Stolzenberg, D'Alessio, and Eitle, 2004).

Recent research continues to examine the relationship between racial threat and policing. For instance, Sever (2001) examines the minority threat-police strength relationship for more than 1100 cities with 25,000 or more residents. He uses two-stage least squares regression models to examine the racial threat hypothesis. Consistent with prior research (for example Jackson 1986, 1989), he finds that percent black has a strong, curvilinear relationship with police strength. He also examines the relationship between other minority populations and police strength but finds less consistent relationships. Therefore, he concludes that the effect of percent black on policing is unique. Another study took a unique approach to assessing the racial threat-police strength relationship. Kane (2003) examines changes in police deployment within particular police districts in New York City in relation to changes in the minority population. He argues that previous tests have all examined the issue of minority threat at the city level. It could be that changes in minority populations affect policing only within particular districts. He uses a pooled time series design for 74 precincts in 1975, 1982, and 1992. He finds that percent black did not effect deployment, but percent Latino did. Interestingly deployment was low until 23% Hispanic then became much higher. He says this could be threat or it could be Hispanic clout. He also finds that changes in crime also affected changes in police deployment within the city, which supports the rational choice perspective discussed above.

Organizational Imperatives

Recent research has also begun to suggest that police strength is likely driven by factors internal to the police organization. This notion comes from consideration of the police agency as an organization. Based on organizational research one would expect that changes in police strength will likely be incremental (increases or decreases) from year to year. Thus, the locus of control over police staffing would primarily rest with the police chief. Several studies find, not surprisingly, that previous police strength is a strong predictor of current police strength (Brandl, Chamlin, and Frank, 1995; Chamlin and Langworthy, 1996; Nalla et al., 1997), but this is true of nearly all social variables and therefore offers a relatively atheoretical explanation of changes in policing.

In sum, there seems to be general agreement that conflict theories better account for variation in state crime control responses than rational choice models (for example Greenberg et al., 1979; Jacobs, 1979; Liska et al., 1981; Liska et al., 1985). Yet, Isaac and Kelly (1981) argue that a significant problem with social control research is the failure to consider politics. Rational choice theorists assume that public policies are the result of the aggregation of citizen interests; conflict theorists assume that conventional politics will be ineffective in garnering important resources for the poor or racial minorities; organizational perspectives suggest that policing is internally determined. Thus, institutional politics tends to be ignored because conflict theorists assume that conventional politics is completely ineffective—leaving protest as the only option (see for example Fording, 2001; Isaac and Kelly, 1981; Jacobs and Helms, 2001; Piven and Cloward, 1971)—whereas rational choice theorists assume that politics operates in the general public interest, leaving no middle ground to be explained. Yet, research evidence suggests that local politics can play a role in determining the allocation of city resources to policing. For instance, Levitt (1997) finds that police hiring is more closely related to whether it is a mayoral election year than crime rates, which McCrary (2002), confirms in a re-analysis of Levitt's data.[3] Thus, it appears that police strength research would benefit from further consideration of the role of politics. In the next section I discuss research on the relationship between local politics and policing.

POLITICS AND POLICING

The consideration of politics and policing has a long but erratic history. For example, Wilson (1968), in his widely-cited discussion of variation in styles of policing, suggests that police department aggressiveness and mission orientation are related to the local political culture (determined mainly from political structure). Wilson argues that police departments adopt one of three organizational styles (watchman, legalistic, or order maintenance), depending on cues from the local political environment. In particular, he focuses on whether the city government is "reformed", meaning a professional administrator controlled the city rather than an elected mayor. He suggests that professional city managers are likely to hire police chiefs in favor of "professional" law enforcement, and thus are expected to adopt a legalistic style of policing. Cities dominated by partisan politics are more susceptible to interest groups, and as a consequence, will try to avoid irritating important groups of voters, adopting the watchman style. Wilson (1968) finds that police aggressiveness in making arrests for minor offenses varies according to the political systems he identified across 146 cities. Therefore, he argues, "...that if any one of the elements of municipal reform is present (nonpartisan or the council-manager form), the political culture becomes more conducive to the legalistic style (Wilson, 1968: 274-275)." Since that time a number of studies have examined the link between local political culture and styles of policing. For instance, consistent with the original study, Wilson and Boland (1978) found that cities with professional city managers issued more citations for traffic violations than cities with elected mayors. A few other studies also found links between styles of policing (at least for minor offenses) and local politics (Crank, 1990; Langworthy, 1985; Slovak, 1986). Langworthy (1986) also finds that local political systems are associated with some differences in police organization, but suggests that the differences were limited, and concluded that political culture didn't appear to be a major constraint on police organizational behavior.

Although this led to a shift away from examining politics in explaining police organizations, recent research has begun to once again consider the relationship between local politics and variation in police organizations. For instance, Wells, Falcone, and Rabe-Hemp (2003) examine the determinants of police organizational features such as number of ranks, centralization, percent civilian, and number of sworn officers for approximately 175 agencies in Illinois, including the form of government as a predictor. It finds no effect of form of government on number of ranks, centralization, density, percent civilian, and number of sworn officers but does find that mayor-council cities have significantly more law enforcement style indicators (stings, asset forfeitures, drug task forces, gang units, SWAT units). These findings are interesting in light of Wilson's arguments. If aspects of policing may be susceptible to politics, it may be that highly visible organizational features such as the creation of a gang unit or a SWAT team are most susceptible to political influence. These are things that a politician can point to as a very specific response to public concern over crime to garner votes. A similar study by Hassell, Zhao, and Maguire (2003) re-examines Wilson's political culture and police organization study. They note that Wilson's argument is one of the most widely cited but least studied. Operationalizing political culture as professional, traditional, and mixed-the authors find minimal support for the effect of political culture on the number of ranks, number of rules and regulations, number of functions performed by special units, and centralization. They note that, rather than abandoning Wilson's theory more research is necessary to clarify the relationship between politics and policing.

Others also suggest that politics is important to consider in explaining police organization behavior. For instance, in their review of the police organization literature, Maguire and Uchida suggest

(2000, p.533), "The structure of city governance, together with local political culture, also continues to have a significant effect on police organizations, suggesting that any comprehensive theory of police organizations needs to account for political effects." Similarly, Koper and Moore (2001, p.32), in a survey of police executives nationwide, find that almost two-thirds of police executives in large department and nearly half of police executives in small agencies agreed that local elected officials or changes in political leadership influenced police staffing. Thus, it seems necessary to consider politics in studies of police strength.

Measures of local politics have also been included in a few recent studies of police strength. For example, two studies of the effects of unionization on police employment and wage levels include form of government (Chandler and Gely, 1995; Trejo, 1991). Yet, these analyses, which focus on unionization, do not include many of the variables identified in previous police strength research. In addition, they only include form of government, which as will be elaborated in chapter 3 is only one element of local politics likely to affect public policies. Likewise, Sever (2001) finds that form of government is not a significant predictor of police strength. Yet, his results may be due to a limitation in his specification of form of government. He uses dummy variables to capture aspects of form of government. Unfortunately, his excluded reference category means that he is not comparing elected mayors to city managers but both of these to commission style governments. Because only a small number of cities had this form of government in 1991 (approximately 11), the analysis probably did not have enough power to detect differences in police strength associated with different forms of government.

Despite the inclusion of local political measures in a few recent studies of police strength, no studies focus mainly on politics, nor do they include more than one local political system characteristic. Thus, I argue that a fuller consideration of the effects of local politics on police strength is warranted.

SUMMING UP

Crime rates vary tremendously across cities. Studies have examined the relationship between city-level crime rates and many social and economic factors such as poverty, family disruption, and ethnic heterogeneity, usually consistent with social disorganization theory. Until recently, however, attention to the role of politics in this process has been limited. Recent advancements in social disorganization theory suggest the desirability of considering the relationship of the community with the city government in determining the ability of communities to organize themselves against crime. Research discussed in the next chapter suggests that cities politically vary in important ways that are likely to affect the ability of citizens to pressure the city government for action, which I argue is likely to affect crime rates.

In addition, numerous studies have examined variation in crime control at the city level, often focusing on changes in police employment. These studies have been motivated primarily by the differing predictions of rational choice and conflict theories. Rational choice theories suggest that crime control policies are mainly driven by changes in the crime rate. Conflict theories suggest that crime control strategies are related to the threat from either racial/ethnic minorities or the economically marginalized. Likewise, the organizational inertia argument suggests that changes in policing are predominantly internally determined. None of these perspectives seriously considers the possibility that the allocation of city resources for criminal justice will be affected by local political system characteristics. Yet, research discussed in the next chapter, suggests that police staffing levels across cities may vary systematically by the structure of the local political system.

Research on crime and policing has begun to consider the role of politics. Yet, what is missing is a theory of how and why local politics and crime, and local politics and policing should be related. In chapter 3, I argue that political resource theory can offer a blueprint for the kind of theory necessary to link city politics and criminal justice outcomes such as crime rates and police strength.

Notes

1. Nolan (2004) did note, however, that when the cities were grouped by population size that the strength of the relationship varied somewhat.
2. Studies, however, are mixed on whether more police means less crime (see Sherman, 2002 for a discussion).
3. Mccrary (2002) takes issue with Levitt's (1997) other claims in the paper, arguing that the weighting scheme used in the paper overestimated the effect of police hiring on crime. He notes, however, that the evidence of an election cycle in police hiring is strong and important in its own right (See also Levitt's 2002, response).

CHAPTER 3:

Institutional Resources, Crime, and Police Strength

It is reasonable to think of crime as a social problem likely to prompt responses from the city government. Given this, it makes sense to consider the structures and processes that are likely to affect city political responses to public policy issues. Although research on crime rates or police strength has not focused much on variation in local politics, it has been the subject of a voluminous body of research in political science. For example, research (discussed below) has examined how local politics affects the representation of ethnic and racial minorities and women on city councils and in the mayor's office, public policy, and voter turnout. There is also a voluminous body of political sociological research that has examined how politics affects policy outcomes, often in relation to national and state variation in welfare policy (for example Hicks and Misra, 1993; Huber, Ragin and Stevens, 1993; Jenson, 1990; Korpi, 1989; Korpi and Palme 1998 Orloff and Skocpol, 1984; Weir and Skocpol, 1985). I argue that a theory derived from welfare state research, Hicks and Misra' (1993) *political resource* theory can provide insights into the ways that local politics should be expected to affect crime and police strength at the city-level.

The discussion in this chapter will proceed as follows: First, I review political resources theory. This discussion will suggest the kinds of structures and processes that should be examined in considering the effects of politics on public policy outcomes. Then, I review political science research that has examined the relationship

33

between local political system characteristics and representation in local government, as well as the effect of political system variation on public policy outcomes. Then, I apply the insights of political resource theory and research on the effects of local political systems to develop an *institutional resource* perspective on crime, and derive some hypotheses regarding the relationship between city politics, social disorganization and crime. Following that I apply this institutional resource perspective to policing to derive some testable hypotheses on the relationship between local political systems and police strength.

POLITICAL RESOURCE THEORY

Studies have examined both the history of welfare state formation (for example Amenta and Carruthers, 1988; Amenta, 1998; Amenta and Halfmann, 2000; Cauthen and Amenta, 1996; Orloff and Skocpol 1984; Weir and Skocpol, 1985) and current variation in welfare state programs (for example Allan and Scruggs, 2004; Hick and Misra, 1993; Huber, Ragin, and Stephens, 1993; Kittel and Obinger, 2003; Korpi and Palme, 1998, 2003). This research generally comes from Neo-Marxist (for example O'Connor, 1973), pluralist (for example Wilensky, 1975), or statist perspectives (for example Orloff and Skocpol, 1984). Neo-Marxists argue that elite interests predominantly shape welfare state policies and that welfare state programs do little to alleviate inequality. Pluralist formations stress the role of partisan politics in shaping welfare policies. [1] Statists stress the role of state institutional capacity and the (partially) autonomous interests of state actors in determining the shape of welfare state policies. Much scholarly debate has centered on the relative strengths of these perspectives, but studies have often shown partial support for more than one theory (Hicks and Misra, 1993; Huber et al., 1993). The development of welfare state perspectives reached somewhat of an impasse by the early 1990s. In response, Hicks and Misra (1993) developed a partial synthesis of these theories, which they refer to as *political resource* theory.

Political resource theory combines elements of state-centered, class-centered, and pluralist theories (Leicht and Jenkins, 1998). According to political resource theory, state institutions provide the context in which various groups shape state policy formation. Within this framework, one is able to consider state and non-state actors, bureaucratic and political structures, and levels of economic activity. Hicks and Misra (1993) argue that resources empower actors to realize their perceived interests. Thus, welfare state policy is the result of a process in which state and non-state actors pursue their perceived interests in welfare policy on the basis of the political resources available to them. Drawing on Rogers (1974), Hicks and Misra (1993) argue that there are two broad categories of resources, instrumental and infra-structural. Instrumental resources are those wielded by particular actors in pursuit of their goals. An example of this would be votes. Citizens can pool their votes to support one political candidate whose views they agree with, thus affecting the shape of state policy. Infra-resources are broader resources that are potentially available to all actors. An example of an infra-resource is the overall democratic political structure or generalized revenue raising capability of states, which can be used in various ways.

Recent Research on Politics and Policy

Although originally developed to explain cross-national variation in welfare state policy, the political resource approach has been applied to a number of different research questions at the national (Hicks and Misra, 1993), state (Leicht and Jenkins, 1998), and local levels (Van Dyke and Soule, 2002). Recognizing that the structure of political institutions matter for policy, a number of studies have used this approach to examine the historical development of public policies, particularly welfare state programs. For instance, Amenta and Halfmann (2000) examine variation in the development of Works Progress Administration (WPA) across the United States. They argue that both favorable institutional settings and actors pushing for a policy are necessary before a generous welfare policy will be developed. They suggest that only open political systems with attendant extensive political rights and programmatically oriented parties (i.e. not patronage based) favored the expansion of the WPA. Thus, to have a well developed social policy program such as a generous WPA, one needs the structural conduciveness of an open and competitive political system combined with democratically leaning legislators, and in some cases strong unions or social. Similarly, Quadagno (2000) examines the integration of hospitals as a case study of power resources and the welfare state. She argues that the reason that hospitals became racially integrated following passage of the Civil Rights Act, particularly as rapidly as they did, was because of a combination of factors. First, hospitals were redefined as public rather than private institutions. This made them subject to federal oversight. Second, federal funds for hospital construction were withheld unless hospitals complied with integration. Yet, this legal change did not have a major impact until the passage of Medicare, a program designed to provide health care for the elderly. Hospitals needed the revenue from Medicare but couldn't get the funds until they certified that they were integrated. The Medicare offices also had the institutional capacity to make sure that hospitals actually complied with the rules to receive the money. So the first key was to redefine hospitals as public so the federal rather than state governments had oversight. Still, that was not enough to force integration. The NAACP had to use the courts to challenge the segregationist policies. Even that was not enough until the power of the purse was invoked in the form of Medicare. Thus, the author suggests that the courts (and public opinion which had begun to favor integration-outside the South) can provide resources for groups to push for equality and redistributive policies.

Consistent with the political resource focus on how politics constrains action, studies have also examined the link between political systems, resources and social movement activity. For example, Soule and Olzak (2004) examine which states ratified the ERA in terms of social movement activity, public opinion, and political systems. They argue that previous studies have suggested that the success of social movements will be based either on the quality of social movement organization, or a favorable political environment regardless of movement strength. Soule and Olzak (2004) suggest that political systems (along with allies in the government) mediate the effect of organizational strength on social movement success. They find that the likelihood of ratification of the ERA in a particular state depended on public support for the ERA and the degree to which political parties in the state were relatively competitive (as opposed to one-party dominating the legislature). Thus, the success of social movements in influencing state action is based on social movement strength combined with favorable political contexts.[2]

Similarly, Leicht and Jenkins (1998) draw on political resource theory in their state-level analysis of public venture capital programs in the United States from 1975 to 1989. They argue that the specific societal interests and specific infrastructural conditions in states promote direct intervention such as public venture capital programs. Leicht and Jenkins (1998) analyze the lower 48 states and treat adoption of the program as a discrete process in the year of its adoption from 1975 to 1989 ($N = 720$). Their results indicate that the adoption of these programs was not the result of class power or political institutions alone, but combinations of the two, suggesting it is important to consider both actors and institutions.

Although political resource theory has not generally been used to examine criminal justice outcomes (cf. Soule and Van Dyke 1999), I believe that political resource theory highlights the ways that politics, particularly the way political systems constrain or enable actors to meet their interests, can matter for criminal justice outcomes such as those discussed in chapter 2. Therefore, I argue that political resource theory can also be applied to the study of city-level institutional politics and crime. It is assumed here that one issue that is very likely to confront city officials is crime, but the perception of crime as a social problem, and the ways that cities deal with it, will vary in important ways that are likely to be structured by available political resources. As noted above, political systems can be an important infra-resource that constrains the kinds of action available to actors. In the next section, I discuss the history and consequences of 19th and early 20th century urban political reforms. This will suggest both the elements of city political systems to consider and that local political variation is likely to matter for crime and policing.

CITY POLITICAL SYSTEMS: THE LEGACY OF REFORM

From the perspective of political resource theory the structure of the political system is an important infra-resource. Therefore, it makes sense to consider patterned variation in urban political systems. A large research literature in political science has examined the causes and consequences of progressive era reforms (See Banfield and Wilson, 1963; Fox, 1977; Griffith, 1974; Hofstadter, 1955 for overviews of the history of reforms). Historically, patronage politics was the predominant model for city government (Banfield and Wilson, 1963). In the patronage system, local officials exchanged political favors for votes. Beginning in the late 1800s and early 1900s, reformers tried to reduce the impact of patronage politics through reforms to the structure of city political systems (Bridges and Kronick, 1999; Knoke, 1982). I focus here on the three most widely-instituted reforms. One major reform was to alter the city's form of government from an elected mayor to a professional city manager appointed to the chief executive position, normally accompanied by an elected city council.[3] The second major change was to alter the means by which council members were elected. In reform cities, council members are elected by voters throughout the city, rather than voters from particular geographical areas. This is known as an at-large system. The third major reform was to remove party labels from elections. Non-partisan elections were designed to remove the party machines that predominated in the 19th Century. Table 3.1 describes the central elements of the three major types of political system variation discussed below. Throughout the rest of the book, to avoid any normative connotations associated with the term reform, following Stucky (2003), I use the term 'traditional' local political systems to refer to mayor/ council forms of government, partisan elections, and district-based city council election systems.

Numerous studies in political science have examined the impact of local political system variation resulting from these reforms on factors such as the representation of ethnic and racial minorities and women, voter turnout, and public policy (for example Bledsoe and Welch, 1985; Engstrom and McDonald, 1981, 1982; Hajnal and Lewis, 2003; Jones, 1976; Karnig, 1976, 1979; Karnig and Walter, 1977, 1983; Karnig and Welch, 1979, 1980, 1982; Lyons, 1978; Robinson and Dye, 1978; Sass and Mehay, 1995; Sass and Pittman, 2000; Welch and Bledsoe 1986, 1988; Welch, 1990; Wood, 2002; Zax, 1990). In the following sections, I first discuss the relationship between local political systems and the representation of minorities in city government. Then, I discuss the effects of variation in local political systems on public policy.

Table 3.1. Traditional and Reformed Local Political Systems

FORM OF GOVERNMENT	
Traditional	
Mayor/ Council	chief executive is elected
Reform	
Council/ Manager	chief executive is appointed professional administrator
Commission	chief executive is group of elected officials
ELECTORAL SYSTEM	
Traditional	
District	council members elected based on geographical area within city
Reform	
At-large	all council members elected by whole city
PARTISANSHIP	
Traditional	
Partisan	party labels used in campaigns
Reform	
Non-partisan	political labels not used in campaigns

Reform and Representation

Perhaps the most widely studied question in urban politics is what effect progressive era reforms had on minority representation in city government, particularly on city councils. City council seats are generally filled in one of three ways. District systems refer to those where city council seats are tied to a particular geographic area within the city. In at-large systems voters from all parts of the city may vote for a candidate. Finally, cities can have mixed systems referring to a combination of district and at-large seats. Early research suggested that district systems facilitate greater minority, particularly African American, city council representation (for example Bledsoe and Welch,

1985 Karnig, 1976, 1979; Karnig and Welch, 1980, 1982; Robinson and Dye, 1978). In fact, some have suggested that 19th Century reforms were as much about limiting the political clout of minority, poor, and immigrant groups as producing a professional government (Bridges and Kronick, 1999; Hofstadter, 1955). Particularly, in southern cities, reform was a tool to minimize or eliminate black political representation. In fact, the exclusion of African Americans from at-large city councils was so prevalent that court cases challenged their constitutionality (see Bullock and MacManus, 1993). At-large systems tend to favor upper class, and to a certain extent, Republican interests, because at-large campaigns tend to be more expensive, require greater name recognition, greater organizational ability, and tend to depress voter turnout (Welch and Bledsoe, 1986). Consistent with this, Scarrow (1999) argues that at-large elections encourage party slate voting because people don't have enough information about the candidates that are not from their area.

Recent research continues to show differences in minority representation based on how council members are elected. For example, Zax (1990) examines the link between district elections and city council representation for blacks and Hispanics in 602 cities with 5% or more black population. He finds that district nominations and elections increase black representation. Mixed systems have somewhat less equitable representation of blacks than district systems, and black representation is worst in purely at-large systems, even controlling for socio-economic factors. Similarly, Engstrom and McDonald (1993) find that at-large systems produce about 30 to 40% of descriptive representation for blacks. Welch (1990) suggests that the effects of electoral systems on minority city council representation declined in recent years. Thus, black under-representation on city councils in at-large cities is not nearly as pronounced as it was in the 1970s. Largely in response to significant pressure from civil rights litigation, many cities have abandoned purely at-large electoral systems, often replacing them with mixed systems. Welch (1990) notes that mixed systems have fairly decent representation of minorities in the district portion of cities, but representation of blacks in at-large seats is actually worse than it previously had been. Sass and Mehay (1995) also find that district elections still enhance black representation equity, especially in the South, but the difference declined somewhat from 1981 to 1991, which they suggest may be due to declines in racially polarized voting. Consistent with this Haeberle (1997), in a case study of Birmingham, Alabama, finds that the court ordered switch to district council elections increased descriptive representation for African Americans and candidates appeared to alter their campaign messages to appear more attuned to district concerns. Finally, Sass and Pittman (2000) re-examine the effect of electoral systems on descriptive representation of blacks on city councils. They find several important trends from 1970 to 1996. First, district elections provide greater black representation in relation to the percent black in a city but that power weakened from 1970 to 1990. In other words the benefit of district elections over at-large elections decreased over the twenty-year span. In addition, black representation in at-large cities in the South increased from 1970 to 1990. However, the trend stagnated in the early to middle 1990s. The authors conclude that the increase in black representation has stagnated and district cities still get higher representation than at-large cities. Other research (for example Sass, 2000; Zax, 1990) has examined the effect of districting on Hispanic representation and finds less of an effect on Hispanic city council representation, which may be due to less residential segregation among Latino voters. The research evidence discussed above suggests that black representation on city councils is greater in cities with purely district electoral systems than cities with at-large representation.

Prior research has also shown that partisanship of elections can also have important consequences for minority representation on city councils, as well as voter turnout. Non-partisan elections tend to make races more candidate-centered, taking attention away from important political issues (Welch and Bledsoe, 1986). Because voters do not have party cues to follow in voting, name recognition is much more important in non-partisan elections. Therefore, non-partisan elections favor candidates with greater resources who are able to gain greater name recognition. In addition, non-partisan elections have been shown to have lower voter turnout (Karnig and Walter, 1977, 1983). This means that higher-income voters are likely to be even more over-represented in local elections. In partisan electoral systems, political parties provide an important organizational resource that minorities can use to mobilize voters. In non-partisan elections this resource is not available. All of these things hurt minority and poor groups' ability to organize effectively because they take away important cues for voters.

Recent research also shows that form of government influences voter turnout. For instance, Hajnal and Lewis (2003) examine voter turnout in 386 cities in California, and find that cities with elected mayors have higher voter turnout. Similarly, Wood (2002) finds that the more political the city, the higher the voter turnout. Cities that are more administratively run (for example city manager) have much lower voter turnout, which he argues is because of the diffusion of power in these cities. In other words, there is no one person that voters can hold accountable. The evidence suggests that political systems, especially partisanship of elections, affect voter turnout (For research on how city characteristics affect other form of political activity see Kelleher and Lowry, 2004).

Local electoral systems can have a number of effects on representation. First, in district and partisan systems, minorities can have more success in running candidates for office, leading to greater physical representation of minorities on councils or in mayor's offices, which some research, suggests can have policy implications (for example Karnig and Welch, 1980). Second, in district electoral systems, minority and poor voters have a more direct tie to their representative in government regardless of race. Thus, the ability of these groups to force the local government to hear their concerns will be greater, because continued tenure in office is directly tied to satisfying the local electorate. Third, in partisan electoral systems, poor and minority voters will have fewer impediments to organization. Party systems impose less of a burden on voters to organize effectively because existing party structures can be utilized. Therefore, minority and poor groups will have less difficulty organizing and becoming a voice in government. Thus, the evidence from political science research is that variation in local political systems can have important consequences for direct and indirect political representation of poor and minority groups.

Reform and Public Policy

The urban politics research discussed above suggests that variation in local electoral systems can affect the likelihood of minority political representation on city councils. Although this is an important finding in its own right, it is also reasonable to wonder whether variation in local political systems from progressive era reforms also affects public policy. Many studies have examined the question of whether reform affects governmental outputs. In the next few sections, I will discuss research on the relationship between urban political reforms and fiscal policies, municipal employment opportunities for minorities, and responsiveness of the local government.

Reform and Fiscal Policy

A number of studies have examined whether taxation and expenditure levels are related to whether the city has a traditional or reformed government. In one of the earliest studies of this type, Lineberry and Fowler (1967) examine the relationship between political system variation and taxation and expenditure levels in 200 cities with 50,000 or more residents in 1960. They find that socio-economic cleavages have consistently larger effects on tax and spending levels in traditional cities. In other words, minority groups have more of an impact on policy in unreformed cities. They use the term responsiveness to refer to this phenomenon. Their general conclusion is that the more reformed a city is the less responsive it is to political pressure. Consistent with this Karnig (1975), in an analysis of 417 cities with 25,000 or more residents in 1960, finds that the relationship between civil rights group mobilization and the adoption of a number of civil rights reforms is stronger in traditional cities. Therefore, he concludes that Lineberry and Fowler were correct and the responsiveness of city governments to groups within the city is lower in reform cities. Similarly, Lyons (1978) argues that cities with mayor-council structures are more likely to be responsive to calls for more spending than council-manager or commission governments because the head of the city government is elected and must satisfy the local electorate to maintain office. Thus, he suggests that calls for increases in city services are more likely to be heeded in mayor-council cities than council manager cities with no elected head of government, or commission cities which are lead by a group of officials, leaving no specific person for the voters to hold accountable.

Other research disputes the link between reform and spending. For instance Liebert (1974) argues that prior studies of expenditures have been highly misleading because they compare overall expenditures without taking account of the variation in functional responsibility. He notes that cities vary tremendously in the things they are functionally responsible for. Some cities are responsible for most aspects of urban services whereas in other areas the county is the major organizational entity. Control over education, hospitals, highways, and especially welfare can vary between local, county, state and federal control. He also suggests that functional control may be related to the level of reformism. He argues that more governments with greater functional responsibility were less likely to have reformism. He partially replicates Lineberry and Fowler and concludes that reformism no longer mediates the link between social cleavages and output.

Similarly, Morgan and Pelissero (1980) find that reformed cities do not spend significantly less than unreformed cities in a matched comparison of 22 cities that changed structures versus those that didn't between 1948 and 1973. They compare spending in 8 categories for the five years before and after a change in the reform structure of the government. They conclude that political structure does not have an impact on local policy, at least with respect to spending. This study appeared to have a major influence on this area of research because studies of reform and spending differences across cities became relatively uncommon after this one was published.

One recent study suggests that perhaps both positions may be correct. Ruhil (2003) argues that there is no reason to believe that form of government should have a linear or permanent effect on spending. He finds that changing to a council manager government does reduce spending in the short run but this effect declines over time. Thus, after about 15 years council-manager and mayor-council cities would be expected to have similar expenditures levels.

Other studies also continue to find differences in spending relating to political system variation, but suggest that these differences may be conditional. For instance, Strate, Wolman, and Melchior (1993) find that there is an election-year oriented tax cycle in mayor council cities but not in council-manager cities. Similarly, Wolman, Strate and Melchior (1996) find increases in spending following a change in the mayor only in mayor-council cities. They did not find shifts in spending priorities but they did find that the changes in expenditure levels were bigger in mayor-council cities where the person defeated an incumbent rather than someone who was retiring. Nunn (1996), in a pooled cross-sectional time series analysis for seven cities in Texas and Indiana, finds that spending for highways, sanitary systems, and water supply was greater in council-manager cities.

Other research suggests that city council electoral systems may affect only certain types of spending. Langbein, Crewson, Brasher (1996) argue that spending differences between district and at-large cities will depend on whether the benefit is concentrated geographically or benefits the city as a whole. District cities will favor spending increases where there is a divisible benefit whereas at-large cities will favor spending increases where the benefit goes to the whole city. Thus, the type of policy considered will determine whether district elections will have an effect. They argue that previous studies of overall spending have been limited since there is no way to know whether total spending is universal or geographically distributed. Langbein and colleagues (1996) suggest that district elections automatically represent the interests of geographically concentrated constituents-which are usually the poor and minorities. Therefore, district elections will produce more outcomes that are universally desirable but locally unwanted, such as schools and community centers (recall that Peterson et al., 2001 suggest that recreation centers reduce crime). Similarly, Wong (1988) suggests that the ability of organized interest groups to affect *redistributive* spending is reduced in cities with reform political systems (which other research shows is related to lower crime rates). Finally, Sharp (1991) argues that the extent to which local economic distress drives economic development policies will be mediated by the degree to which the local government is accessible to public demands. In particular she argues that reformism reduces government accessibility and therefore will weaken the link between unemployment and economic development policies. In a 1984 survey of local city administrators she finds fairly consistent support for the idea that accessibility leads to greater economic development policy in the face of need. She suggests that part of this may come from the desire of local officials to claim credit for the economic initiatives in order to gain political advantage. Thus, the weight of the evidence suggests that some kinds of spending in a city vary based on whether the political system is traditional or reformed. In the next section I examine the link between local political systems and minority public employment.

Reform and Minority Public Employment
One prominent question is whether the physical representation of African Americans in city government translates to any tangible benefits for that group such as increased employment opportunities (Eisinger, 1982). Because public employment is one outcome that the city government is likely to have a relatively large influence on, numerous studies have examined the relationship between minority political representation and minority public employment. Studies have examined the link between race and employment (Alozie, 1999; Behr, 2000; Dye and Renick, 1981; Eisinger, 1982; Kerr and Mladenka, 1994; Mladenka, 1989b; Santoro, 1995), Hispanic/ Latino ethnicity and employment (Alozie and Ramirez; 1999; Mladenka, 1989a) and female representation and public employment (Kerr, Miller, and Reid, 1998; Sass and Troyer, 1999).

Although not unequivocal (cf. Alozie, 1999; Mladenka, 1991; Santoro, 1995), the weight of the evidence suggests that local political systems affect the ability of minorities to gain political employment. For instance, Dye and Renick (1981) examine the factors that affect African American employment in city jobs in 42 cities with at least 10% black population. They find that the percentage of black representation on the city council is a strong predictor of black employment in police and fire jobs. Interestingly, it is not numbers in relation to the population that is important but raw number on the council. In other words, it isn't the equity of representation but the raw strength of numbers that seems to matter. This relationship is also true for Hispanic representation as well.

Other studies suggest that the effects of local politics on municipal employment may be conditional. For instance, Mladenka (1989b) examines the factors that explain black and Hispanic municipal employment and finds that political systems interact with the presence of minority representation to affect minority city employment and this effect varies by region. In the South, the strongest predictor of black city employment was black city council presence but only in district cities. Black city council presence did not enhance black municipal employment in at-large cities. In the West a different pattern emerged, such that African American city council presence increased black municipal employment only in at-large cities. He attributes this to the lack of segregation in western states which he argues, likely leads to coalition building as opposed to district based concerns.

Other studies suggest that the race of the mayor matters for public employment. Numerous studies have examined the likelihood of minorities obtaining the chief elected officials post (for example Alozie 2000). The ability of minorities to gain the mayor's office is an important symbol of political clout for the minority community, and contains the potential for substantive representation and benefits for the minority community as well. The policy impact of having a minority mayor has also been studied (for example Browning, Marshall, and Tabb, 1984; Campbell and Feagin, 1975). For example, Eisinger (1982) studies 43 cities in 1973 and 1978 and finds that black population is the biggest predictor of black employment. He finds a small but significant effect of black mayors on prestigious city jobs, but no effect of black city council representation on city jobs. Similarly, Salzstein (1989), in a study of 136 cities with 5% black and at least 100 full-time sworn officers in 1970, finds that black mayors significantly predict increases in full-time sworn black officers as well as the adoption of citizen review boards of police action. Alozie (1999), in a study of 121 cities with 5% African American or Hispanic populations finds that minority mayors enhance police employment for both groups. On the other hand, Kerr and Mladenka (1994), in a pooled time series study of 65 cities, find that both black city council presence and black mayors had an influence on black police employment but only in traditional cities. Similarly, in a study of New Orleans from 1978 to 1997, Behr (2000) finds that having a black mayor and a black controlled city council led to increases in black municipal employment.

Thus, it appears that both the characteristics of local political systems as well as who occupies offices matters not only symbolically for the representation of minorities but also provides tangible benefits in terms of expanded municipal employment opportunities. In the next section, I discuss the relationship between local political systems and the susceptibility of city governments to political pressure.

Reform and Responsiveness
Finally, urban politics research has examined the openness of political systems to political pressure. Recall that Lineberry and Fowler (1967) argue that traditional systems are more open to input from interest groups within the city. Some research has examined this issue. For instance, Hansen (1975) examines the linkages between elite views of city issues and citizen views of social issues. She calls agreement between elites and citizens 'concurrence'. Thus, when both city leaders and citizens consider the same issues important, there is greater concurrence. She argues that citizen participation can have two kinds of effects on elite behavior. First, the fear of being thrown out of office can cause leaders to try and respond to popular demands. Second, citizen participation can influence leaders' behavior by communicating citizen preferences. Hansen argues that there are certain conditions that are likely to enhance citizen-elite concurrence, specifically: electoral competition, traditional political systems, and citizen participation. She finds that concurrence is greater in cities with partisan elections and in mayor-council cities, and where elections are competitive (partly a function of voter turnout, in turn a function of partisan elections). She also finds a relationship between SES and concurrence. Generally, elites and upper income groups appear to see community issues similarly. Partisan cities appeared to increase the concurrence of elites and lower and middle-income groups, which she attributes to the communicative function that voting plays. Hansen (1975:1198) concludes that certain political factors "… may give lower status citizens a better chance to influence their leaders." In general, it appears that citizen-elite issue priority agreement is greatest under conditions which favor citizen input into local politics.

Similarly, Shumaker and Getter (1983) argue that the question of "who gets what" in the prior research on city expenditures is somewhat simplistic. They argue that a better question is "who gets which things they want", which they call responsiveness. Shumaker and Getter (1983) argue that the local policy makers are (perhaps not surprisingly) more responsive to advantaged groups, a situation they call responsiveness bias. They survey local politicians in 51 communities regarding responsiveness of the local government to groups in the city. Shumaker and Getter (1983) find that city income is related to responsiveness toward advantaged groups. They also find that reformed city governments are less responsive to the demands of all groups in the city, which may be an indirect result of reformism making the organizational bases of groups weaker. In other words, reformism depresses party organization, voter turnout, and favors Republicans, which indirectly reduces responsiveness to minority and poor interests. On the other hand, greater party competition (more common in traditional cities) increases the responsiveness of local officials to disadvantaged groups. Leaders of any party must be more responsive to their constituents when party competition is increased. Thus, the degree to which poor and disadvantaged groups can get their concerns heard in local government depends on how the local political system constrains or enables interest group action.

In a recent study, Sharp (2002) suggests that local political system variation also affects the responsiveness of local officials to so-called "morality issues" such as gay rights and pornography. She finds that form of government mediates community pressure for action on these issues. Specifically, mayors were more likely to take action on morality issues in response to group pressures. Similarly, in recent studies of political systems and economic policies, Feiock, Jeong, and Kim (2003) argue that the council-manager form of government insulates the government from political pressure. They argue that political pressures on elected mayors may cause them to adopt less efficient economic development policies in order to take advantage of credit claiming opportunities. Finally, Feiock (2004) finds that form of government influences which "second generation" land use policies are adopted in Florida counties. In both cases, however, the authors argue that this "insulation" may be a good thing when it comes to economic development policies because political pressures may create incentives for elected officials to adopt less efficient but politically popular alternatives (i.e. getting tough on crime and the prison boom). This suggests that form of government matters but that it may be a two edged sword—sometimes political influence can lead to inefficient policies. The larger point, however, is to suggest that political systems matter and they affect the ability of interest groups to make their voices heard in local government.

The research discussed above suggests that local political systems do matter for political representation of minorities and substantive policies such as minority public (particularly police) employment opportunities, as well as affecting the agreement between local officials and citizens on policy priorities and the ability of citizens to affect the political process and ultimately both economic and non-economic policy outputs. Thus, local political systems matter for public policy generally. What has not been discussed to this point is how this relates to crime and police strength. In the next section, I apply these insights to develop an institutional resource perspective on crime and police strength.

INSTITUTIONAL RESOURCES AND CRIME

Political resource theory emphasizes that social and political outcomes are the result of how various groups use available resources to pursue their interests. I argue that political resource theory can provide some valuable insights into the kinds of structures and processes that are likely to shape the ability of the local community to organize against crime. The previous discussion of political resource theory suggests that local institutional politics can be a resource for groups to gain political representation and that variation in local political systems affects local public policies. I argue that this variation in representation will be associated with the ability of poor and minority groups to have their concerns addressed by the city government. One important concern that citizens are likely to have is crime. City political systems are likely influence the ability of citizens to make the local government respond to their desire to reduce crime. If "concurrence" on local issue priorities is related to whether the city government is traditional or reformed, then the agreement of city officials and citizens on crime as a priority may likewise depend on the local political system. In other words, cities with traditional governments are expected to be more attuned to citizen concerns regarding crime. In addition, they are likely to respond by increasing police forces.

Thus, theories of crime and police strength discussed in chapter two would benefit from considering, how local political systems affect the responses of city officials to crime and citizen concern over crime. I call this focus on politics and criminal justice an *institutional resource* perspective. The institutional resource perspective focuses on both sides of the equation—community characteristics *and* the way city political systems facilitate or inhibit the voicing of citizen concerns over crime. Thus, the perspective incorporates both institutional political resources and community-level context and resources to explain variation in crime and police strength. In this section, I outline this perspective in greater detail and derive some testable hypotheses regarding the relationship between local politics and crime.

Social Disorganization

As discussed in Chapter 2, social disorganization theory has frequently been used to explain variation in city-level crime rates (Miethe et al., 1991). Structural factors such as poverty, unemployment, and family disruption are thought to make the maintenance of informal social ties more difficult, resulting in weaker informal social control, which ultimately leads to higher crime rates. The assumed mechanism is informal control but city-level studies do not usually have the data to assess this issue due to the difficulty and expense of collecting information on informal control in large numbers of cities. Therefore, they examine differences in crime across cities with different patterns of structural indicators of social disorganization. Extant research suggests considerable empirical support for the relationship between structural indicators of social disorganization and crime – cities with greater poverty, family disruption, urbanization, and ethnic heterogeneity are more likely to have higher crime rates (for example Kubrin and Weitzer, 2003; Land, et al., 1990; Parker, 2004; Parker and Johns, 2002; Parker and McCall, 1999; Sampson, 1987; Sampson and Groves, 1989; Velez, Krivo, and Peterson, 2003). Following social disorganization theory, my first hypothesis is: *Social disorganization will be associated with higher crime rates.*

Form of Government

One can think of the structural indicators of social disorganization in terms of resources. Poverty, family disruption, and ethnic heterogeneity inhibit the ability of communities to generate community ties and informal social control. Therefore, one could say that these communities lack resources for social organization. As discussed in Chapter 2, previous social disorganization research has focused mainly on *internal* community dynamics. Recent advancements in social disorganization theory suggest that *external* community dynamics can also affect social disorganization processes (Bursik and Grasmick, 1993; Clear, Rose, Waring, and Scully, 2003; Guest, 2000; Kubrin and Weitzer, 2003; Rose and Clear, 1998; Velez, 2001). The institutional resource perspective would suggest that infra-structural and instrumental resources available to communities are likely to affect their ability to organize against crime. Urban politics research suggests that one infra-resource available to communities is the local political system. Therefore, it is possible that the resources available for community organization will vary depending on the nature of the city's political system.

City form of government is one source of local political variation that has been posited to have a direct effect on crime. Wilson and Boland (1978) argue that commission and city manager governments are more insulated from group demands (see also Feiock, 2004; Feiock, Jeong, and Kim, 2003; Sharp, 2002). City managers do not depend on voter support for continued job tenure and commission governments have no clear head of government. Therefore, citizens have less leverage in trying to impact the style and policies of the police than in mayor/council governments where the continued tenure of the chief elected official depends on maintaining voter support. With less leverage, one might expect more negative police-community relations. Indeed, some research supports this. For instance, Jacobs and Wood (1999) and Jacobs and Carmichael (2002) find higher rates of interracial violence in cities with lower political efficacy among blacks.

If decreased political efficacy follows from the reduced responsiveness to citizen groups in cities with a professional city manager, then this could lead to higher rates of violence. Because mayors face election campaigns, they must also consider whether organized groups could be swing votes. The pressure to address interest groups in the city is likely to be lower for city managers or commissioners, who are more likely to address city-wide needs. Lyons (1978) suggests that calls for increased city services may get more attention in mayor-council cities. If true, these services might aid poor and minority areas in organizing against crime, which Velez (2001) argues could lead to greater public control and reduce crime. Thus, to the extent that city governmental form inhibits responsiveness of the police to organized pressure from citizen groups, this could have a negative impact on police community relations, negating one of the infra-resources that would available in mayor/ council political systems and increasing crime. Thus, *ceteris paribus*, mayor-council cities could be expected to have lower crime rates. Therefore, my second hypothesis is: *Cities with mayor/council structures will have lower crime rates than those with council/manager or commission governments.*

Partisanship of Elections

Another potential infra-resource is the structure of the local electoral system. The prior discussion suggested that representation of poor and minority groups on city councils is greater (Welch and Bledsoe, 1988) and voter turnout is higher (Alford and Lee, 1968; Karnig and Walter, 1977, 1983; Wood, 2002) in partisan systems. Partisanship also appears to increase the link between citizens and elites, making elites more attuned to citizen issues priorities (Hansen, 1975; Shumaker and Getter, 1983). Consequently, partisanship of elections and the way city council members are elected should operate analogously to form of government. If, as Wilson and Boland (1978) suggests, the accessibility of the local government is related to police practices and accountability then one would expect that local governments that facilitate citizen involvement should be more responsive and have lower crime. Velez (2001) also argues that the ability of communities to secure public resources should be tied to lower crime rates.

Therefore, if partisan cities facilitate citizen preferences to the local government, then ceteris paribus, partisan cities should have lower crime rates. Thus, my third hypothesis is: ***Cities with partisan elections will have lower crime rates.***

District v. At-Large City Council Election

The third source of variation in local governments from progressive era reforms is the method of electing city council members. Extant research suggests that minority group representation on city councils is enhanced with district-based elections (Sass and Pittman, 2000; Welch, 1990; Welch and Bledsoe, 1988; Zax, 1990). Research has been somewhat less clear on the policy implications of district-based elections, but Welch and Bledsoe (1988) find that council members in district-based elections see their district as their constituency, whereas council members elected at large consider voters across the entire city. Although research has not considered variation in crime across cities with different city council election procedures, there are reasons to expect it might affect crime. For instance, Bledsoe (1986) finds that cities with district-based elections have greater black political efficacy and Jacobs and Wood (1999) find that this is associated with lower interracial violence. If district based elections, and the attendant increases in representation lead blacks to feel their actions will matter, this could lead to increased community organization which Rose and Clear (1998) argue is likely to reduce crime. Thus, if minority political efficacy and responsiveness to district-based concerns are greater in district cities, it could reduce social disorganization and consequently, crime.

District-based elections may also increase the likelihood of redistributive spending by maximizing interest group organization according to Wong (1988). Recent research suggests that redistributive spending is related to reductions in violence. For example, DeFronzo (1997) finds that homicide rates are lower in cities with higher AFDC benefits (see also Hannon and DeFronzo, 1998; Pratt and Godsey, 2003). Therefore, my fourth hypothesis is: ***Cities with district electoral systems will have lower crime rates than cities with at-large or mixed elections.***

Interaction of Disorganization and Politics

In addition to these direct effects of local political system characteristics, I argue they are likely to have important consequences for the relationship between social disorganization and crime. As discussed in Chapter 2, Rose and Clear (1998) argue that there is important variation across communities in political organization and the ability of the community to interact with the government to solve community problems (see also Triplett, Gainey, and Sun, 2003). As Rose and Clear (1998) point out, not all poor communities are unable to organize politically. They suggest that residents' sense of political efficacy is one important source of variation in political organization. Research on local political systems, discussed above, suggests some important structural reasons why some poor and minority communities may be more able to organize than others. To the extent that there are structural facilitators to organization, communities are likely to have a higher sense of political efficacy as they see that they can impact the local government. Indeed, based on data from the 1976 National Election Studies, Bledsoe (1986) found that district-based elections were associated with higher political efficacy for blacks. In other words, blacks are more likely to feel they have a say in local government in cities with district-based elections than at-large elections. In addition, Marschall (2004), in a study of Detroit, finds that parent teacher association (PTA) and neighborhood crime watch participation rates are higher in areas with higher political efficacy. This variation in organizational ability and local political efficacy is likely to have important consequences for the structural factors previously associated with social disorganization, such as socio-economic status, social mobility, family disruption, ethnic heterogeneity, and urbanization. For example, city services such as trash removal and road maintenance can support property values, reducing mobility. Or, citizen activity in local government may produce needed resources in the community to ameliorate poverty or limit family disruption. In addition, research suggests that mayor/ council city government are likely to be more amenable to calls for more services (see Lyons, 1978). To the extent that cities are responsive to the needs of their poorer citizens, citizens will be more able to combat the structural conditions of social disorganization, increase community strength and reduce crime. Also, recall Velez (2001), who finds that the most disadvantaged communities are the ones that benefit most from increases in public control.

Finally, Stucky (2003), in a negative binomial regression analysis of cities with 25,000 or more residents in 1990, finds that the effect of disadvantage on violent crime depends on the form of government. Disadvantage had a smaller effect on violent crime in cities with elected mayors than in cities with appointed managers. Therefore, local form of government is an important infra-resource that is likely to affect the relationship between structural indicators of social disorganization and crime rates. This prediction can be formalized in hypothesis five: *The effect of social disorganization on crime rates will be lower in cities with Mayor/council forms of government.*

Cumulative Effects of Political Systems on Crime

It also stands to reason that if individual local system characteristics can enhance political representation, combining them should have an effect on crime as well. Thus, as the number of traditional political system characteristics increases, representation of poor and minority interests should be greater and crime should be reduced. As the degree of reform goes up, the responsiveness to political pressure goes down (Lineberry and Fowler, 1967). Thus, the degree to which a city can be characterized as reform or traditional is also likely to be related to the crime rate. This suggests my sixth hypothesis: *Cities with more traditional political systems will be associated with lower crime rates.*

Recent research also suggests that economic and non-economic institutions interact with social conditions to produce variation in crime rates. Studies in the institutional anomie tradition suggest that the effect of economic factors on crime is related to politics. For instance, Maume and Lee (2003) find that the relationship between inequality and homicide across counties depends on political factors such as voter turnout, which is consistent with Chamlin and Cochran's (1995) state level analysis showing that the relationship between poverty and crime depends on voter turnout. As noted, research shows that partisan elections increase voter turnout. Therefore, one might expect the relationship between poverty or inequality and crime to be lower in partisan cities. This may be because cities with traditional political systems are more susceptible to political pressure and attuned to citizen issue priorities (for example Hansen, 1975; Sharp, 2002; Shumaker and Getter, 1983). Because extant research shows that political institutions and the economy interact to affect crime, it seems reasonable to expect that aspects of local political variation will interact with the economy as described above to affect crime. Thus, my seventh hypothesis is: *As the number of traditional local political system characteristics increases, the effect of social disorganization on crime will decrease.*

Race of the Mayor

Another potential instrumental resource is the race of the mayor. Some research suggests that the race of the mayor can have policy implications (for example Karnig and Welch, 1980). Specifically, minority political leaders have been found to be similar in socio-economic status to whites but tend to be more liberal in their views on social welfare policies than whites. Therefore, to the extent that minority mayors are able to have an effect on policy, social welfare policies should be favored in cities with minority mayors or council members. Research also suggests that African American mayors are more likely to institute civilian review boards for police (Salzstein, 1989), which may enhance police-community relations. In addition, recall that Jacobs and Wood (1999) show that black violence against whites is lower in cities with Black mayors. Jacobs and Carmichael (2002) find that violence against police is also lower in cities with African American mayors, which they argue could be the result of reduced feelings of injustice and increased political efficacy (Bobo and Gilliam, 1990) in the minority community. Thus, black mayors may produce better relationships between the police and the Black community as well as reducing feelings of injustice, which should lead to lower crime rates. This suggests my eighth hypothesis: *Cities with black mayors will have lower crime rates.*

INSTITUTIONAL RESOURCES AND POLICE STRENGTH

An institutional resource perspective can offer insights into the study of police strength as well. Given citizen concern over crime, there is a strong likelihood that cities will see it as a social problem that must be addressed. It is assumed here that one likely city response to citizen pressure to reduce crime is to increase the number of police. The first question to be addressed is the extent to which city officials see crime as a pressing issue. As discussed in Chapter 2, the rational choice perspective suggests that the perception of the seriousness of crime will be primarily related to the officially recorded crime rate. If changes in city priorities occur in response to a rational aggregation of citizen interests, then it is reasonable to expect that greater citizen concern with crime will lead to greater city resources being applied to crime control. Therefore, my ninth hypothesis is: *Police strength will be positively associated with crime rates.*

Conflict and Police Strength

Recall from chapter 2, that conflict theories argue that state policies are not the result of the rational aggregation of citizen interests. Rather, conflict theorists suggest that changes in police employment will be related to the perceived threat to elite interests posed by economic or ethnic/ racial minorities and the ability of these groups to pressure city officials. Neo-Marxists argue that increases in the number of unemployed are likely to be perceived as a threat by economic elites. Economic conflict theories suggest my tenth hypothesis: *High unemployment will be associated with increased police employment.*

Similarly, following Blalock (1967), a number of studies have suggested that official social control efforts are tied to the perception of minority threat, which in turn, is related to the overall size of minorities in an area (Jackson and Carroll, 1981; Jackson, 1986, 1989; Jacobs, 1979; Sever, 2001, 2003). Thus, my eleventh hypothesis is: *City minority populations will be related to police employment.*

Local Political Systems and Police Strength

The institutional resource perspective adopted here, however, suggests that both the rational choice and conflict views of state action are limited. Rational choice perspectives assume that public policies are in the general public interest. An institutional resource perspective suggests that public policies are the result of how groups use available resources to pursue their goals. Therefore, public policies will vary depending on the ability of various groups to press their concerns, and are not always congruent with the general interests of the public. The ultimate shape of crime control policies will be the result of how city political systems constrain or enable certain groups to pursue their interests in anti-crime policies.

Similarly, an institutional resource perspective suggests that conflict theories are limited as well. Whereas conflict theories suggest that the state reflects the interests of racial or economic elites, an institutional resource perspective suggests that under certain circumstances state institutions can be an important resource for poor and minority groups to advance their interests. Under democratic governments the economic weakness of the poor can be transformed in certain circumstances to political power through the numerical strength of workers. Yet, the ability of poor and minority groups to affect the political process is related to the structure of local political systems. Therefore, I argue that local political system characteristics will be related to police employment. Police strength is expected to vary based on form of government, partisanship of elections and the way city councils are elected.

An institutional resource perspective suggests that the perception of crime as a social problem by city officials will also be based on the ability of certain groups to press their concerns with the city. Therefore, the perception of the seriousness of crime, and corresponding official responses will be based in part on objective social and economic conditions noted above, but also on the relative strengths of various actors and how they pursue their perceived interests. I also assume that city actors have interests somewhat independent of solving these problems (see Block, 1987 for a discussion of the potentially autonomous interests of state actors).

Numerous studies have argued that electoral competition boosts government responsiveness to social issues (for example Barrilleaux, 1997; Dawson and Robinson, 1963; Dye, 1966; Holbrook and Van Dunk, 1993; Key, 1949; Barrilleaux, Holbrook, and Langer, 2002). Thus, city political responses to crime will depend on whether those in authority are elected or appointed and the kinds of impacts that minority and poor constituents can have on the electoral process. Previous research has suggested that the city political system characteristics discussed above are an important resource that can facilitate or inhibit the ability of citizens to voice their concerns and impact the political process. I discuss below a few specific ways in which actors and interests will structure crime policy determination, including city fiscal capacity, and city institutional political structures.

One important source of variation in a city's ability to deal effectively with social problems is overall fiscal capacity. Fiscal capacity is an important infra-resource that constrains city responses to social problems. A number of previous studies of crime control have examined the effects of city revenue (for example Chamlin, 1989, 1990; Jackson and Carroll, 1981; Jackson, 1986, 1989). Yet, these studies include fiscal capacity mainly as a control variable. They do not relate fiscal capacity theoretically to the other types of resources that affect police strength. Regardless of the motivation, it is important to consider the overall resources available in relation to the resources devoted to policing. Therefore, my twelfth hypothesis is: *Cities with greater fiscal capacity will have greater police strength.*

As discussed above, there is likely to be institutional variation in the ability of citizens to press their demands with city officials. The discussion focused on three forms of local political variation outlined in Table 3.1. Form of government, city electoral systems, and the partisanship of elections are all expected to affect the ability of citizens to affect the political process. Therefore, if crime is a general concern among city residents, it is reasonable to expect that this concern will be more readily translated into changes in police employment in cities with political structures that enhance participation by the poor and ethnic and racial minorities. It may also be that political factors affect mayors and city managers differently. Recall that several authors have suggested that mayors are more susceptible to public pressure (Feiock,

2004; Sharp, 2002; Wilson and Boland, 1978). It seems reasonable to believe that mayors may be likely to use increasing the number of police on the streets as a way to enhance re-election campaigns. Consistent with this, Choi, Turner, and Volden (2002), in a study of 209 cities from 1993-1997, find that mayor-council cities were almost 40% more likely to request federal grant money for community policing officers than council-manager cities.

Other research suggests that it is reasonable to expect city council electoral systems and police employment to co-vary. For instance, Mehay and Gonzalez (1994) examine the relationship between city council electoral systems and the power of unions to affect municipal employment policy. They argue that the costs of influencing city council members will be lower in district systems and therefore municipal employees will be better able to affect municipal employment conditions, especially in the presence of a union. They find that at-large cities have lower about 10% lower police employment. Thus, city council electoral systems affect police employment levels. This suggests the following hypotheses regarding the relationship between local political systems and city formal social control: *Cities with mayor/ council governments will be associated with higher police employment* (H13). *Partisan cities will be associated with higher police employment* (H14). *Cities with district based elections for city council will be associated with higher police employment* (H15).

In addition, if individual traditional local political system characteristics can be expected to have an effect on police strength, it makes sense that the combination of these structures in cities should have an effect as well. Therefore, my sixteenth hypothesis is: *Cities with more traditional system characteristics will be associated with higher police employment.*

Strength of the Mayor

As discussed above, there is variation across cities in form of government. Even within the broad types of political systems discussed in Table 3.1, there is some variation from city to city. For example, one source of variation is the strength of the mayor. In strong mayor cities, mayors have broad power over city budgets, veto power over city council resolutions, and broad powers of appointment. In weak mayor cities, mayors do not have these powers (Engel, 1999; Svara, 1990). An institutional resource perspective suggests that the strength of the mayor is likely to have an impact on the kinds of policies that are implemented. If mayors face significant pressure from the citizenry, it stands to reason that mayors with broader power will have more of an impact on policies. Therefore, even controlling for the form of government, I expect that cities with strong mayors are likely to have higher police employment, all else being equal. Thus, my seventeenth hypothesis is: ***Strength of mayor will be associated with police employment.***

SUMMING UP

Local politics has received relatively little attention in extant city-level studies of crime and police strength. Yet, political resources theory suggests that the kinds of resources available to groups will structure the ability of these groups to pursue their interests. Thus, there is reason to expect that variation in the resources available to groups will affect their ability to organize against crime and to force the city to respond to their concerns. One important resource from this perspective is the structure of local government. Urban politics research suggests that there is important variation in the ability of groups, especially the poor and ethnic minorities to gain political representation based on the institutional structures of local governments, and that variation across city political contexts affects public policy outcomes. I use these insights to begin to develop an institutional resource perspective on crime and crime control, and derive testable hypotheses that will be assessed in Chapter 5 and 6. In the next chapter, I describe the data and methods that will be used to test these hypotheses.

Notes

1. Recent research has been somewhat ambivalent on the role of partisan politics, however. For instance, Korpi and Palme (2003) and Allan and Scruggs (2004) find that variation in partisan politics across advanced industrial countries affects the strength of welfare state programs, particularly in terms of recent "retrenchment." In contrast, Kittel and Obinger (2003), claim that the role of partisan differences has declined somewhat in recent years.
2. See Ingram and Rao (2004) for a discussion of how social movements and political activities affected anti-chain store legislation.
3. Although council-manager cities retain a mayor position, he or she is usually selected from among the council members and serves a largely ceremonial function.

CHAPTER 4:

Study Methodology

This chapter discusses the data and methods used to evaluate the hypotheses generated in chapter 3. Studies of crime have been done at the SMSA, city, county, state, and national level (see Land et al., 1990 for a review). Therefore, an important consideration is the most appropriate unit of analysis. Given the theoretical predictions of the institutional resource perspective regarding the impact of local political systems on crime rates and police strength, it seems logical to choose cities as the unit of analysis. I argue that cities are an appropriate unit of analysis for several reasons. First, cities are real political entities that make decisions regarding the allocation of resources to fight crime. Also, city-level analyses of both crime and police strength are common. Therefore, the current results can be compared with the results of prior studies. Finally, neighborhood-level political information is simply not available on a large number of cities. Therefore, for example, examination of variation in political efficacy across neighborhoods cannot currently be undertaken for cities with 25,000 or more residents.

In collecting data to assess my hypotheses, I attempted to include as many cities as possible and use the most recent data available. Information on cities with 25,000 or more residents is available from the U.S. Census Bureau in its *County and City Databook* series (U.S. Department of Commerce, 1984, 2000). The most recent year for which all relevant social and economic data are available for cities is 1990 (at the time of data collection). Therefore, the dependent variables—crime rates and police strength—are measured in 1991. This provides a one-year lag for most variables corresponding to the hypothesized causal ordering of the constructs. A few variables are measured in 1989 or 1991 where that is the only information available, and any deviations from the one-year lag structure are noted on a case-by-case basis. The details of variable construction are discussed below.

In addition, for purposes of replication, I report the results of analyses using analogous 1981 data. The measurement of these variables is identical to 1991 with the exception of a ten-year lag, unless otherwise noted. Thus, for example the natural log of the population in 1990 is included in the analyses reported on 1991 data and the natural log of the population in 1980 is included in the analyses reported on 1981 data. In order to make the research samples for 1981 and 1991 comparable, the universe of cities for both studies is cities with 25,000 or more residents in both 1980 and 1990.

DATA SOURCES

The analyses reported in Chapters 5 and 6 employ data from several sources. Crime rates and police employment data were obtained from the FBI Uniform Crime Reports data (U.S. Department of Justice, 2000a, 2000b). Information on city political systems comes from City Form of Government (FOG) surveys conducted by the International City/ County Management Association in 1981, and 1991 (Urban Data Service, 1982, 1992). These surveys contain information such as the form of city government, and electoral rules for city council members, as well as characteristics of mayors and city council members. In addition, various economic and social characteristics of cities come from the *County and City Databooks* (U.S. Department of Commerce, 1984, 2000). The discussion will proceed as follows: First, I compare the current sample with the population of cities with 25,000 or more residents in both 1990 and 1980. Then, I describe the sources and measurement of the crime, police, demographic and political data used in the analyses in chapters 5 and 6.

Comparing the Sample with the Universe of Cities with 25,000 or More Residents

Although some demographic information is available for all cities with populations of 25,000 or greater in both 1990 and 1980, non-response to the FOG survey reduces the number of cases somewhat. For example in 1991, 821 cities with 25,000 or more residents responded to the FOG survey, while in 1981, 869 cities responded. In addition, missing data on certain demographic variables of interest reduces that number somewhat. Therefore, one concern is the extent to which the cities used in the analyses are representative of the universe of cities with 25,000 or more residents. Tables 4.1 and 4.2 compare the universe and sample means and standard deviations of some demographic variables for cities used in the analyses reported in

Table 4.1. Population and Sample Means for Analyses Reported in Chapter 5.

Variable	1991 Cities 25,000+	1991 Sample	1981 Cities 25,000+	1981 Sample
N	912	717	912	751
Pop.	108855 (311991)	87437 (105657)	100692 (300020)	93856 (279494)
Unemp. %	6.64 (2.75)	6.46 (2.52)	6.44 (2.86)	6.46 (2.90)
% Black	12.73 (16.41)	11.97 (15.06)	11.20 (15.54)	11.48 (15.57)
Med. Inc.	30885.26 (10351.5)	31033.16 (10135.65)	17613.49 (5031.93)	17497.77 (4956.14)
% Poor	13.20 (7.40)	12.86 (7.20)	11.45 (6.23)	11.49 (6.23)
Female HH %	18.80 (7.13)	18.30 (6.57)	16.26 (6.06)	16.40 (6.07)
Pop. 5-17 %	17.04 (3.42)	17.04 (3.46)	19.56 (3.67)	19.37 (3.52)
% HS Grads	76.88 (10.23)	77.63 (9.62)	70.06 (11.62)	69.92 (11.50)

Note: Standard errors in parentheses.

chapters 5 (Table 4.1) and 6 (Table 4.2). In general, the samples of cities, used in the analyses reported in subsequent chapters, are quite comparable to the universe of cities with 25,000 or more residents. The percent black, median income, percent poor, percent unemployed, percent of female-headed households, percent of population age 5-17, and percent of high school graduates are all quite similar. Therefore, the samples appear to be representative of the demographic makeup of the universe of cities with 25,000 or more residents. The only exception is that the cities in the sample have slightly smaller populations on average than the population of cities with population 25,000 or more.

Table 4.2. Population and Sample Means for Analyses Reported in Chapter 6.

Variable	1991 Cities 25,000+	1991 Sample	1981 Cities 25,000+	1981 Sample
N	912	715	912	790
Population	108855	89415	100692	85652
	(311991)	(110715)	(300020)	(155008)
Unemp. %	6.64	6.50	6.44	6.40
	(2.75)	(2.54)	(2.86)	(2.84)
% Black	12.73	11.99	11.20	10.81
	(16.41)	(15.01)	(15.54)	(15.01)
Med. Inc.	30885.26	30797.89	17613.49	24153.58
	(10351.5)	(9893.13)	(5031.93)	(6766.03)
% Poor	13.20	12.97	11.45	11.36
	(7.40)	(7.07)	(6.23)	(6.23)
Female HH %	18.80	18.37	16.26	16.15
	(7.13)	(6.59)	(6.06)	(5.87)
Pop. 5-17 %	17.04	17.03	19.56	19.39
	(3.42)	(3.43)	(3.67)	(3.58)
% HS Grads	76.88	77.61	70.06	70.31
	(10.23)	(9.56)	(11.62)	(11.41)

Note: Standard errors in parentheses.

VARIABLES USED IN THE ANALYSES

In this section, I describe the measurement of the variables used in the analyses reported in subsequent chapters. Specific variable construction is the same for the analyses reported in Chapter 5 and Chapter 6, unless otherwise noted. Prior research has suggested that skewness of variables can be problematic in city-level studies of crime (Land, et al., 1990), especially studies such as the current one, which includes cities with as few as 25,000 and as many as 7 million residents. Therefore, univariate statistics were examined closely and variables were natural log transformed where appropriate to meet the assumptions of least squares regression.

Dependent Variables

Crime
The current study measures crime as the crimes known to the police from the Uniform Crime Reports (UCR) data. Following standard practice in criminological research, and to facilitate comparison across cities, I use the rate of index offenses per 100,000 city residents. Index crimes include: murder, rape, robbery, aggravated assault, burglary, larceny, and auto theft. There has been a long-standing debate within criminological circles regarding the validity of the UCR data. A number of studies have suggested that organizational imperatives of police departments and differences in reporting across jurisdictions limit the validity of the UCR statistics (see Levitt, 1998 for a discussion). In addition, numerous studies have compared the UCR data to the National Crime Victimization Survey (NCVS) (Blumstein, Cohen, and Rosenfeld, 1991; Jensen and Karpos, 1993; McDowall and Loftin, 1992; Menard, 1992; O'Brien, Shichor, and Decker, 1980). These studies suggest differences between the UCR and NCVS in crime rates at various points in time as well as some differences in trends in crime. Therefore, some early studies recommended the NCVS over the UCR data. More recent studies, however, have suggested that neither is inherently superior (Blumstein, et al., 1991, 1992; Jensen and Karpos, 1993; McDowall and Loftin, 1992). Therefore, the advisability of using one or the other data source should be made on a case-by case basis.

There are several good reasons for using UCR data in this study. First, most studies suggest that for serious crimes, the UCR is a reasonably accurate reflection of crime (for example Gove, Hughes, and Geerken, 1985; LaFree, 1998).[1] Second, the UCR is the indicator of crime that is most likely to be used by cities in determining of the need for changes in police strength. Third, it is the indicator that has been used most frequently in both city-level crime and crime control studies. Therefore, the comparability of the current study with the results of other studies is enhanced. Finally, city-level data for the range of cities in the sample is simply not available from the NCVS. Therefore, the UCR is the only available measure of crime for the cities in the sample.

Previous studies of variation in crime across cities have focused on a number of aspects of crime. Some examine murder exclusively (for example Bailey, 1984; Messner and Golden, 1992; Parker, 2004; Parker and Johns, 2002; Parker and McCall, 1999; Peterson and Krivo, 1993; Shihadeh and Ousey, 1998). Others examine violent crime (for example Shihadeh and Steffensmeier, 1994; Shihadeh and Flynn, 1996) or combinations of violent and property crime (for example Miethe et al., 1991). The institutional resource perspective outlined above provides no a priori reason to expect that variation in local political systems will affect one type of crime more than others. Therefore, chapter 5 examines variation in the Part I index crime rate in 1991 (and 1981 in supplemental analyses). In addition, the Part I index crime rate in 1986 (or 1976) is included to reduce the likelihood that unobserved heterogeneity across cities could affect results. The inclusion of the lagged value of the dependent variable also allows for a stronger test of the effects of the covariates in the model because most of the variation in the dependent variable will be explained by the prior crime variable. As Loftin and McDowall (1982: 395) note ... "Granger [1969] argues that if one variable (X) causes another variable (Y), then X should provide a more accurate prediction of Y's present value than could be obtained by using past values of Y alone." Thus, if the independent variables included in the analysis are significantly related to the current value of the dependent variable, controlling for the lagged value of the dependent variable, then they can be said to Granger cause crime. Marvell and Moody (1996) also discuss Granger causality in a recent study of police employment and crime rates.

In chapter 6, the Part I index crime rate in 1989 (1979 for the supplementary analyses) is included as an independent variable. It is assumed here that there is a two-year lag in the effect of crime rates on the number of police due to the length of time it takes for city budgets to change and police officers to be trained in reaction to changes in the crime rate.

Police Strength
Prior police strength research has used a number of indicators. Some research examines variation in police expenditures (for example, Jackson 1986, 1989; see also Sever, 2003). Other research examines police employment. I chose to use police employment rather than police expenditures for several reasons. First, with respect to the crime rate equations in chapter 5, based on rational choice perspectives, variation in the number of police employed could certainly explain variation in crime. If the actions of the police prevent crime, then it is reasonable to expect that the number of police officers in a city will be related to the crime rate. Second, citizen concern over crime is most likely to translate into calls for "more police on the streets." Third, changes in expenditures, may lead to changes in the number of police or they may be used to increase police salaries or purchase equipment, which are less likely to be directly related to crime.

I focus here on the number of sworn police officers rather than the total number of police employees for three reasons. First, sworn officers represent the bulk of most police departments. Second, sworn officers are the ones most likely to have an impact on the crime rates as they are the ones most directly involved in social control, unlike for example, clerks or ticket writers, who support the activities of the police but do not directly generate reports of crime or arrests. Finally, I focus on sworn police officers because citizens typically concern themselves with the number of police on the street. Therefore, changes in the number of sworn officers are most likely to change in response to citizen pressure for more police.

Because this variable exhibits skewness, the natural log of the number of sworn police officers per 1000 city residents in 1991 (1981 for supplementary analyses) is included as an independent variable in chapter 5. This variable is measured concurrently with the crime rate variable, which raises the issue of causal order. In other words, one could argue that the crime rate influences the number of police officers rather than that police officers influence the crime rate. Yet, even if this were the case, the effect of crime on changes in policing is not likely to be instantaneous. Cities make budgets at least a year in advance and training police officers takes time. Therefore, there is a low likelihood that the number of police in 1991 is caused by the crime rate in 1991. I argue that it is much more likely that the number of sworn police officers in 1991 will affect the number of crimes known to the police. The natural log of sworn police officers per 1000 city residents is also used as the dependent variable in the analyses reported in Chapter 6.

Institutional Resource Variables

The discussion in the previous chapter on the effects of progressive era reforms on urban political and social outcomes primarily focused on three broad changes in city government: form of government, city council election procedures, and partisanship of elections. Therefore, to capture variation across cities along these dimensions, information on city political systems was obtained from FOG surveys conducted in 1991 (1981 for supplementary analyses). All variables relating to city political systems are measured contemporaneously with the dependent variables in chapters 5 and 6. Thus, the issue of causal order arises again. Here again, I argue that it is quite unlikely that the crime rate or the number of police officers in a particular year will be an important factor in cities changing their form of government in that same year. Thus, it is quite unlikely that crime rates or the number of sworn police officers in 1991 actually cause the form of government to change. In addition, local political systems change rather infrequently.

Form of Government
As outlined in Chapter 3, urban politics research suggests that city form of government can have important consequences for political and social outcomes. Therefore, for the analyses reported in chapters 5 and 6, I create a two-category variable indicating a city's current form of government in 1991(1981 for supplementary analyses) called *mayor-council*. This variable is coded 1 for cities with mayor/ council forms of government and 0 otherwise. It is also possible to have town meeting

and representational town meeting forms of government but these systems are very rare and none of the cities in the sample had that form of government. Therefore, I do not discuss them here. This variable was gathered from the FOG surveys (see Appendix A for item wording). Preliminary analyses examined whether a two or three-category breakdown of city form of government was appropriate. Results suggested that the relevant differences are between mayor/ council, on the one hand, and council/ manager and commission governments, on the other.

City Council Election Procedures

Urban politics research also suggests that the rules for electing city council members can have consequences for minority representation on city councils, the link between councilors and their constituents, and even redistributive spending. Above, I argued that this will have implications for crime rates and police strength. To capture variation in city governments along this dimension, I create a categorical variable, using the 1991 (1981 for supplementary analyses) FOG data, named *district*, which is coded 1 if 100% of city council members are nominated and elected in geographical districts, and 0 otherwise (see Appendix A for the exact wording of FOG questionnaire items). Preliminary analyses compared two-and three-category specifications of this variable (i.e. district vs. at-large/ mixed compared to district vs. mixed vs. at-large). Results suggest no differences, and the two-category variable is used in the present analyses for simplicity.

Partisanship of Elections

Extant research also suggests that partisanship of elections is important in a number of ways. First, partisan elections make it easier to organize and influence the political process. Second, partisan elections encourage higher rates of voter turnout (which usually increase participation of poor and minorities disproportionately since the affluent already vote). Therefore, consistent with the institutional resource perspective outlined above, I use the FOG data to create a categorical variable named *partisan*, which is coded 1 if the political party affiliation of candidates appears on ballots in local general elections, and 0 otherwise (see Appendix A for item wording).

FOG survey data were missing for the district and partisan variables for a number of cities in the sample. To reduce the number of missing cases, values of these two variables were substituted from the FOG surveys in 1996 (Urban Data Service, 1997). Thus, if the response to the partisanship or electoral rules question was missing for a city in 1991 and the response was given in 1996, then the value for 1996 was used as the 1991 value. It is assumed that these are the best approximations of the value of the variable in 1991. A similar procedure was employed for 1981 data substituting 1986 values (Urban Data Service, 1986). Because values are substituted for 130 cities in 1991 (120 in 1981) for the partisanship variable, and 125 cities in 1991(112 in 1981) for the district variable, the substitution procedure could affect results. Therefore, models reported in chapters 5 and 6 that included and excluded substituted values were compared. In no case did including substituted values for the partisan or district variables change the substantive interpretation of results.

Traditional Government Index

As noted in Chapter 3, the institutional resource perspective predicts individual effects of local political systems on crime and police strength. It also seems reasonable to expect that the effects of political system variation will be cumulative. Therefore, I use the FOG data to create a continuous variable called *TG (traditional government) index* to capture the cumulative effects of traditional city political system characteristics. The range of this variable is $0 - 3$, depending on the number of traditional political system characteristics in the city. Thus, if a city had a mayor-council form of government, partisan elections, and district-based city council elections, it had a value of 3. If two of the three traditional characteristics were present the value of the variable was 2 and so on.

Strength of Mayor

The institutional resource perspective also suggests that the strength of the mayor may affect the range of influence that a mayor has on public policies, which I argue could have consequences for police strength. Therefore, I used the FOG data to create a categorical variable named *strong mayor*, which is coded 1 if the mayor had control over the budget submitted to city council, and 0 otherwise (see Appendix A for item wording).[2]

Social and Economic Variables

In this section I describe the measurement of the social and economic variables included in the analyses reported in chapters 5 and 6. The variables discussed in this section are all taken directly from the *County and City Databooks* (1984, 2000). In the discussion of each variable, I also note the original data collection agency. Corresponding to the hypothesized causal ordering of the variables, most of these variables are measured one year prior to the dependent variables, unless otherwise noted. In the variable descriptions given below, I discuss variable construction for the primary analyses conducted on the sample in 1991. Chapters 5 and 6 also report results of analyses conducted on 1981 data. Measurement of the variables used in the supplemental analyses using 1981 data are identical to 1991 but with a ten-year lag.

City Expenditures
Previous studies of crime control have often included some measure of fiscal capacity as a constraint on the resources available to fight crime, usually as a control variable (for example Chamlin, 1989, 1990; Jackson and Carroll, 1981; Jackson, 1986, 1989). The institutional resource perspective also suggests that city spending could be an important factor to assess. Therefore, the impact of the amount of revenue that cities spend on residents will be assessed. This variable is measured as city expenditures (in dollars) per resident in 1991 (multiplied by .001 to eliminate leading zeros in results tables), and is taken from the U.S. Census Bureau's Survey of Government, 1991. Here again, the contemporaneous measurement of the independent and dependent variables raises the potential issue of the causal ordering of variables, but it is quite unlikely that crime will have an instantaneous effect on city expenditures, because city budgets take time to develop. Therefore, I argue that it is much more likely that city expenditures influence crime rates than crime influences expenditures in the same year.

City Expenditures for Health and Hospitals, Education, and Welfare
The institutional resource perspective suggests that certain types of city expenditures may be more likely to influence crime rates than others. Consistent with this reasoning, I include a measure of *public spending*, which is the percentage of total city expenditures related to health and hospitals, education, and welfare in 1991, taken from the U.S. Census Bureau's Survey of Government, 1991.

Police Expenditures
To control for variation across cities in the size of police budgets which could affect the number of sworn police officers, police expenditures per capita is included in the analyses reported in Chapter 6. This variable is measured as the total city expenditures (in dollars) allocated to policing, divided by the city population, and is taken from the U.S. Census Bureau's Survey of Government, 1991.

Population Size
Consistent with social disorganization theory, as well as policing research, many previous studies of crime and crime control have included some measure of population size. The rationale is that, as city size increases, the capacity for informal social control decreases, necessitating increased formal social control by the police (for example Jackson, 1986, 1989; Land, et al., 1990; Sampson and Groves, 1989; Velez et al., 2003). Therefore, city population in 1990 (or 1980 for supplemental analyses) is included in the current study, taken from the 1990 census. The natural log transformation of total city population is used to reduce skewness.

Black Population
As discussed in Chapter 2, race is implicated in both studies of crime (for example Parker and McCall, 1999; Sampson, 1985, 1987; Shihadeh and Flynn, 1996; Velez et al., 2003; Wadsworth and Kubrin, 2004) and crime control (for example Chamlin, 1989; Jackson, 1986, 1989; Liska and Chamlin, 1984; Liska, et al., 1981, 1985; Sever, 2001, 2003). Therefore, percent black is included in analyses of both crime rates and police employment. This variable is the percentage of city residents that are African-American in 1990 (or 1980 for

supplementary analyses), taken from the 1990 census. This variable is part of the social disorganization index in the crime rate equations in chapter 5 (creation of this variable is discussed below).

In Chapter 6, the natural log of the percent black is used in analyses reported because the variable exhibits skewness. Since some cities have no blacks in the population, I add a constant to this variable (.0001) to avoid taking the natural log of 0 (which is mathematically impossible).

Poverty

Both social disorganization theory and studies of police strength emphasize the role of economic disadvantage (for example Greenberg, et al., 1979; Liska et al., 1981; Liska et al., 1985; Lowenkamp, et al., 2004; Nalla et al., 1997; Parker, 2004; Sampson and Groves, 1989; Velez et al., 2003). Social disorganization theory sees poverty as a barrier to community organization, whereas conflict theories of crime control suggest that the poor are a potential threat to elite interests. Therefore, poverty is included in the analyses in chapters 5 and 6. This variable is the percentage of city residents with income below the poverty line in 1989, taken from the 1990 census. Because census questions ask about income from the previous year, poverty information from the 1990 census refers to income generated in 1989.

Median Income

Previous studies of city-level crime and crime control have often included median income (Greenberg and Kessler, 1982; Greenberg et al., 1985; Jackson and Carroll, 1981; Jackson, 1989; Jacobs, 1979; Krivo and Peterson, 2000; Swimmer, 1974; Velez et al., 2003). This is a common indicator of economic well-being in a city, and provides an indicator of the tax base of a city. Therefore, consistent with prior research, median income is included in analyses. It is expressed as the median income of city residents (in dollars) in 1989, taken from the 1990 census. This variable is measured in 1989 because the census asks about income generated in the prior year.

Unemployment

Another important economic indicator that has been included in numerous prior studies is unemployment. Recall from the discussion in Chapter 2 that unemployment was implicated in Sampson's (1987) account of the relationship between race, marital disruption and crime. In addition, the discussion regarding conflict perspectives on police strength pointed to the unemployed as a potential threat to economic elites. Therefore, consistent with prior research, unemployment is included in the current analysis, and is the percentage of city residents who are unemployed in 1990, taken from the 1990 census.

Female-Headed Households

Family disruption has long been implicated in city-level studies of crime. Consistent with numerous city-level studies (for example Krivo and Peterson, 2000; Osgood and Chambers 2000; Parker, 2004; Shihadeh and Flynn, 1996; Velez et al., 2003), the percentage of households that are headed by females in 1990 are included as an indicator of family disruption, taken from 1990 census.

Youthful Population

Another control variable often included in city-level analyses of crime is the percentage of the population that is young. Prior research on the distribution of crime across the life course suggests that crime commission rises through the teen years, then declines rapidly from the early twenties on (see Gottfredson and Hirschi, 1990 for a review). Thus, failure to control for the size of the youthful population could mean that differences in crime across cities could be simply due to variation in the size of the population most likely to be involved in crime. Therefore, in chapter 5, to control for the potential that crime varies simply because of variation in the population most likely to commit crime, the percentage of population age 5 to 17 in 1990 is included in analyses, taken from the 1990 census data. This variable is included in chapter 6 as an indicator of another potentially threatening population that may lead to increases in police strength.

Although it is the only indicator of age of a city's population that is readily available for the cities in the sample, the age range included in this study makes sense from a theoretical standpoint as well. Children ages 5-17 are the portion of the population most likely to be affected by variation in informal social control and family disruption. The exact ages included in previous studies vary (compare Bailey, 1984; Messner and Golden, 1992; Peterson and Krivo, 1993; Shihadeh and Flynn, 1996). Land, et al., (1990) suggest, however, that various measures of young population are highly correlated and conclude that the particular operationalization of this concept is not likely to impact results.

High School Graduates
Another variable often associated with social disorganization in previous research is education. One indicator of education used in previous city-level research is the percentage of adults that have graduated high school (Krivo and Peterson, 2000; Velez et al., 2003). Therefore, I include the percentage of adults age 25 and older with high school diplomas in 1990, taken from the 1990 census.

Owner Occupied Homes
Another issue frequently discussed in social disorganization is residential stability. One measure of residential stability included in previous city-level research is the percent of houses that are owner-occupied (Krivo and Peterson, 2000; Miethe et al., 1991; Velez et al., 2003). Therefore, I include the percentage of year round dwellings that are owner occupied in 1990, taken from the 1990 census.

Southern Region
Another variable included in many previous city-level analyses of crime (for example Parker and McCall, 1999; Peterson and Krivo, 1993; Shihadeh and Flynn, 1996; Shihadeh and Ousey, 1996, 1998; Velez et al., 2003) and police strength (Greenberg et al., 1985; Jackson 1986, 1989; Jacobs, 1979; Liska et al., 1981; Sever, 2001) is region of the United States. Early studies suggested that either a Southern or black subculture of violence accounted for higher crime rates often seen in the South (Gastil, 1971 Hackney, 1969; Wolfgang and Ferracuti, 1967). More recently, studies have suggested that structural factors such as unemployment, poverty, inequality and family disruption account for differences in crime across region (for example

Loftin and Hill, 1974; Messner, 1983). Regardless of the underlying mechanism, there are clear differences in crime by geographic region.

Studies have also examined regional differences in crime control at the city level. Regional differences have been attributed to: social relations (Jacobs, 1979), penal philosophies (Murton, 1976), party politics (Glaser, 1996; Key, 1949; Patterson and Caldeira, 1984; Steed, 1997), and minority relationships (Jackson, 1986, 1989; Liska et al., 1981). Although empirical support for the purported effect of region has not been universal, there are good theoretical reasons to expect regional variation in both crime and crime control. I follow established practice in city-level crime and police strength research by including a categorical variable that is coded 1 for cities in southern states and 0 otherwise. Southern states include: Alabama, Arkansas, Florida, Georgia, Kentucky, Louisiana, Maryland, Mississippi, North Carolina, South Carolina, Virginia, and Texas.

STATISTICAL MODELS

I assess my hypotheses regarding crime rates (chapter 5) and police employment (chapter 6) in 1991 using Weighted Least Squares (WLS) regression techniques. Ordinary Least Squares (OLS) regression assumes that error variance is constant. Violation of this assumption can produce inefficient parameter estimates and bias significance tests.[3] A plot of residuals against city population produced a classic cone shape, indicating heteroskedasticity. One solution to this problem is to weight the data. I assume that the error variance is inversely proportional to the population size, and weight the data accordingly. Thus, all reported analyses in Chapter 5 and 6 are WLS regressions. The inclusion of this variable eliminates the appearance of heteroskedasticity in residual plots. It is interesting to note that the substantive interpretations of the political system effects discussed in chapters 5 and 6 are substantively very similar regardless of the model specification. This suggests that the results are robust to model specification. Appendix B contains correlation matrices for variables included in the analyses reported in chapters 5 and 6.

Notes

1. O'Brien (2003) reports that crime rate increases from the 1970s to the 1990s were probably partly an artifact of increases in efficiency of reporting to and by police agencies. This should not pose a problem within the current study because each of the cross-sectional nature of the study. As long as gains in efficiency were relatively constant across agencies, then changes over time will not affect the reported results.

2. Analyses substituting veto power of the mayor and appointment power of the mayor produced substantively similar results those in the models reported.

3. In cities with low crime rates, small absolute changes in crime can represent huge proportional changes. Thus, for example going from 1 homicide to 2 represents a doubling of the homicide rate, whereas going from 99 to 100 represents a much smaller proportional increase. In effect, the residual dispersion can be greater for smaller cities than larger ones, constituting a departure from the homogeneity of variance assumption.

CHAPTER 5:

Urban Politics and Crime

This chapter examines hypotheses regarding institutional resources, social disorganization, and crime rates in 1991. The organization of the chapter is as follows. First, I examine some descriptive statistics based on variation across my sample of cities in local political structures in 1991. Then, I discuss the results of my analysis residuals to check for heteroskedasticity, unduly influential cases, and multicollinearity. Next, I discuss the results of WLS regression analyses in 1991 with the natural log of the overall crime rate per 100,000 residents as the dependent variable. Then, I discuss supplementary analyses that further probe the relationship of institutional resources and crime. Specifically, I discuss analyses that examine the cumulative effect of traditional governments on crime and percent of the city budget allocated to health / hospitals, education, and public welfare. Next, I report analyses that examine the effect of another institutional resource—race of the mayor—on crime in 1991. Finally, I report results of WLS regression analyses for overall crime in 1981 and discuss similarities and differences between the analyses across the two time periods.

DESCRIPTIVE STATISTICS

Table 5.1 presents the overall means of variables broken down by city political system characteristics. This table shows some interesting differences in crime and social disorganization. First, as can be seen by comparing columns A and B of Table 5.1, mayor/ council cities have mean crime rates that are nearly 300 reported index offenses lower per 100,000 residents than city manager and commission cities. This is

83

particularly surprising because the usual structural indicators of social disorganization – such as percent poor, percent unemployed, median income, female-headed households and education levels – would suggest that crime rates should be higher rather than lower. Likewise partisan cities have nearly 200 fewer reported index crimes per 100,000 residents in 1991 than non-partisan cities, despite the fact that the usual structural indicators of social disorganization suggest that crime rates should be higher in partisan cities (see columns C and D of Table 5.1). Yet, partisan cities have lower crime rates in 1986 and 1991. Thus, from a pure social disorganization perspective, the results in Table 5.1 represent a puzzle. Given existing research, one would not expect to see lower crime rates in cities with higher structural indicators of social disorganization, regardless of the local political context.

It is also interesting to note that mayoral and partisan cities have higher expenditures per capita despite having lower median incomes in the city, consistent with Lyons' (1978) prediction that mayoral cities are more responsive to calls for greater spending. In particular, mayoral and partisan cities spend significantly larger proportions of their budgets for public welfare, education, and public health. Mayoral cities spend 13.0% of their budgets on public health, education, and welfare as opposed to only 5.5% in council manager and commission cities in 1991. Likewise, in partisan cities 11.1% of expenditures go to public health, education, and welfare as opposed to only 7.1% in non-partisan cities. Thus, these results suggest that political systems characteristics affect how city budgets are allocated.

The same differences do not appear, however, when comparing cities whose council members are elected by district with those that are not. The right two columns of Table 5.1 compare variable means in district cities with means for cities with mixed and at-large electoral systems. Contrary to the pattern exhibited in mayor and partisan cities, cities with district elections for city council actually have nearly identical crime rates in 1986 and slightly higher crime rates in 1991 than cities with mixed and at-large electoral systems. Thus, city electoral structures do not follow the same pattern as form of government and city partisanship. This pattern is borne out in the regression analyses discussed below. Prior to discussing regression results, it is necessary to determine whether the assumptions necessary for regression analyses are met.

Table 5.1. Variable Means by Political System in 1991.

Political Structure	Mayor/ Council	Council /Man.	Partisan	Non- Part.	District	AL/ Mixed
Column	A	B	C	D	E	F
N	227	464	140	551	139	552
Population	95678	86476	84869	88299	94264	88299
Crime 91	7111.3	7410.8	7162.3	7350.5	7627.4	7233.1
Crime 86	6293.9^{**}	7092.8	6173.5^{**}	6841.1	6787.5	6841.1
SD Index	0.187^{***}	-0.172	0.327^{***}	-0.151	0.217^{***}	-0.122
% Black	14.69^{**}	10.86	17.79^{***}	10.67	16.71^{***}	10.96
% Unemp	7.14^{***}	6.14	7.2^{***}	6.28	7.02^{**}	6.33
% Poor	13.75^{*}	12.5	14.66^{**}	12.47	15.34^{***}	12.3
Med Inc	28813^{***}	31990	28244^{***}	31633	27321^{***}	31859
Fem HH	20.46^{***}	17.35	21.95^{***}	17.47	19.89^{***}	17.99
%HS Grads	74.70^{***}	79.04	73.97^{***}	78.56	76.51	77.92
%Age 5-17	17.03	17.02	16.27^{**}	17.22	17.16	16.99
City Exp/ Capita	943.29^{*}	834.80	961.78^{*}	847.23	847.09	876.32
% HEW	13.04^{***}	5.46	11.14^{*}	7.14	8.63	7.78
PD/1000 Res.	2.03^{***}	1.73	2.16^{***}	1.75	1.93	1.80

Note: $p < .05$, ** $p < .01$, *** $p < .001$.

ANALYSIS OF RESIDUALS

The use of least squares regression techniques rests on several assumptions. Therefore, I performed a thorough analysis of residuals on the models reported in Table 5.2 to determine whether the underlying assumptions of least squares regression appear to be met. As noted in Chapter 3, one of the assumptions of OLS regression is that error variance is constant. Violation of this assumption can produce inefficient parameter estimates and lead to misleading results from significance tests. A plot of residuals against city population for the models in Table 5.2 produced a classic cone shape, indicating heteroskedasticity. As noted, I assume that the error variance is inversely proportional to the population size, and weight the data accordingly. The inclusion of this variable eliminates the appearance of heteroskedasticity in residual plots. Thus, analyses reported in this chapter are WLS regressions.

Another important consideration is the potential that individual cases may unduly influence results. Based on Belsley, Kuh, and Welch (1980) studentized residuals, Dffits, and Cook's D values were computed for all cities in the sample (For a discussion of the criteria used to eliminate influential cases see Appendix B.). The cities listed in Appendix B exhibited extreme values on these criteria and were therefore excluded from reported analyses. The exclusion of these outliers only affected parameter estimates. Sensitivity analyses revealed that the exclusion of outliers did not alter the patterns of significance of results. Otherwise, a thorough analysis of residuals suggests that residuals appear to be reasonably normally distributed, and the expected value of residuals is zero. Thus, it appears that the assumptions underlying least squares regression are met.

Prior research has suggested that multicollinearity can be problematic in city-level studies of crime (for example Land, et al., 1990). Preliminary analyses suggested extreme multicollinearity among the structural indicators of social disorganization used in the analyses in Chapter 5. One measure often used to detect multi-collinearity is the variance inflation factor (VIF). (VIFs) were calculated for each of the variables in the analysis. Neter, Kutner, Nachtsheim, and Wasserman (1996) note that the largest VIF among the independent variables is usually an indication of the severity of multicollinearity and maximum VIFs exceeding 10 indicate severe multicollinearity. Models including percent unemployed, percent black, percent poor, percent owner occupied homes, median income, and percent of households headed by females consistently had maximum VIFs exceeding 10.0.

Principal components analyses produced one factor in 1991 (and 1981) with the following indicators: percent black, percent poor, percent unemployed, percent of high school graduates, percent of owner-occupied homes, median income, and percent of female-headed households. The loadings for all variables are quite high: 0.63 to 0.92. I label this factor social disorganization. I generated factor scores for each city based on the demographic variables listed above. The substitution of factor scores associated with this social disorganization index into regression equations seemed to reduce multicollinearity, as indicated by variance inflation factors dramatically. VIFs were calculated for all analyses reported in this chapter to monitor the possibility that multicollinearity could arise among other variables in the analyses. In no case did the VIFs in the equations reported in chapters 5 and 6 exceed 4.0. Thus, there is no reason to believe that reported results are affected by multicollinearity. In the next section, I examine hypotheses regarding institutional resources and crime for cities with 25,000 or more residents.

WLS REGRESSION RESULTS: CRIME IN 1991

Table 5.2 presents the results of three regression equations predicting the natural log of the rate per 100,000 residents in overall index crimes in 1991. Equation 1 includes several control variables suggested by prior research, including city population, percent Age 5-17, location in a southern state, city expenditures per capita, and police officers per 1000 state population. In addition, all three equations include the natural log of the index crime rate in 1986 to control for potential unobserved heterogeneity across cities. This reduces the potential that results are affected by omitted variable bias. The adjusted R squared value is .800, which suggests that the control variable included in this model account for much of the variation across cities in crime rates (of course, much of this is the prior crime variable). Consistent with expectations, population size is significantly associated with crime in all three equations in Table 5.2. Thus, in general, larger cities have higher crime rates. In addition as expected, cities located in southern states have significantly higher crime than cities in non-southern states, in all three equations in Table 5.2. Contrary to expectations, police

Table 5.2. WLS Regression of Crime Rates on Social Disorganization and City Political Variables in 1991, N=717.

Variable	EQ.(1)	EQ. (2)	EQ. (3)
Constant	1.812***	2.299***	2.455***
	(0.163)	(0.179)	(0.190)
Population (Ln)	0.022**	0.023**	0.027**
	(0.008)	(0.008)	(0.008)
% Age 5-17	0.960***	0.552*	0.592*
	(0.247)	(0.250)	(0.249)
South	0.100***	0.085***	0.080***
	(0.016)	(0.016)	(0.016)
Sworn Off. / 1000 Res. (Ln)	0.296***	0.234***	0.248***
	(0.023)	(0.025)	(0.025)
Expenditures Per Capita	0.005	-0.003	0.003
	(0.015)	(0.014)	(0.014)
Index Crime Rate Per 100,000	0.732***	0.689***	0.666***
Residents in 1986 (Ln)	(0.021)	(0.022)	(0.023)
Social Disorganization Index		0.061***	0.092***
		(0.022)	(0.013)
Mayor/ Council			-0.018
			(0.018)
Partisan			-0.011
			(0.02)
District			0.0003
			(0.018)
Social Disorganization*			-0.059***
Mayor/ Council			(0.016)
Adjusted R^2	0.800	0.810	0.814

Note: N=717, Numbers in Parentheses are standard errors. * p < .05, ** p < .01, *** p < .001.

officers per 1000 residents are actually significantly *positively* related to crime in all three equations in Table 5.2. Yet, this finding is consistent with the findings of some previous city-level crime research (for example Huff and Stahura 1980). Also, contrary to expectations, expenditures per capita are not significantly related to city-level crime rates in any equation reported in Table 5.2. Given the importance ascribed to state expenditures in the institutional resource perspective, this is a troubling result. In subsequent analyses in this chapter, I probe the relationship between expenditures and crime further.

Equation 2 adds the factor score for each city based on the social disorganization index described above. Consistent with numerous prior studies outlined in Chapter 2, structural indicators of social disorganization are significantly positively associated with crime rates $(p < .001)$. Thus, crime is higher when structural factors associated with social disorganization such as poverty, family disruption, and unemployment are higher. Interestingly, the inclusion of the social disorganization index reduces the magnitude of the effect of being in a southern state on crime, although it remains significant. Therefore, higher crime rates in southern cities appear to result, in part, from higher levels of poverty, family disruption, and unemployment in the South.

Equation 3 includes the city political system variables suggested by the institutional resource perspective. Recall that these are categorical variables coded 1 if the traditional government characteristic was present and 0 otherwise. Thus, *mayor/council* refers to cities having an elected mayor and a city council form of government. *Partisan* refers to whether campaigns use political party labels, and *district* refers to whether city council members are elected solely from geographic areas in the city. Contrary to what one would expect from an institutional resource perspective, district and partisan cities were not significantly related to crime rates for cities in the sample in 1991, controlling for the other factors in the model.

Consistent with hypothesis 5, however, the effect of social disorganization on crime depends on the local form of government. The significant negative value $(p < .001)$ for the interaction term between social disorganization and mayor-council means that the structural indicators of social disorganization have less of an impact on crime in mayor-council cities, even controlling for crime and the other variables in the equation. To illustrate this, consider the differences in expected crime in mayor-council versus council-manager and commission cities for a unit increase (approximately a standard deviation for the disorganization index) in the structural indicator of social disorganization. Because the mayor-council variable is a binary variable with a value of 0 in council-manager and commission cities, the interaction term drops out of the prediction equation. Thus, one would expect an increase in the natural log of the index crime rate of .092 (the parameter estimate for the main effect of social disorganization) in council-manager or commission cities, whereas in mayor-council cities one would expect an increase of only .032 (.092 + -.059) in the natural log of the crime rate. Thus, the effect of structural indicators of social disorganization on crime is nearly two-thirds lower in mayor-council cities than council-manager and commission cities. Therefore, it appears that political systems can provide a resource for communities to increase their level of organization and combat the structural barriers to organizing against crime such as poverty, unemployment, and family disruption. In the next section, I further examine the relationship between city expenditures, political system variation and crime in 1991.

Public Spending and Traditional Governments

Given the centrality of expenditures in the institutional resource perspective, the lack of a relationship between overall expenditures per capita and crime is disappointing and warrants further examination. Certainly an institutional resource perspective would suggest that spending should be negatively related to crime, but it is possible that only certain types of city spending are related to crime (see for example Wong, 1988). Therefore, I limited my attention to the types of public spending I thought would be likely to have an impact on crime. The models in Table 5.3 include a measure of *public spending*, which is the percent of the total city budget allocated to health and hospitals, public welfare, and education. I assume that these three types of spending are likely to have a much more direct impact on crime rates and social disorganization than spending for sanitation or highways, for example. Equation 1 includes the control variables included in Table 5.2. The effects of the variables are similar to those reported above. The natural log of the city population, percent ages 5-17, location in a southern state, the natural log of the number of sworn officers per capita, and the reported index crime rates per 100,000 residents in 1986 were all significantly positively associated with the natural log of index offenses per 100,000 city resident in 1991. Equation 1 in Table 5.3 also substitutes public spending, for the expenditures per capita variable included in Table 5.2. Here, public spending for health, education, and welfare, is significantly negatively related to crime ($p < .05$), even

Table 5.3. WLS Regression of Crime Rates on Public Spending and the Traditional Government Index in 1991.

Variable	EQ.(1)	EQ. (2)
Constant	2.409***	2.508***
	(0.183)	(0.192)
Population (Ln)	0.024**	0.026**
	(0.008)	(0.008)
% Age 5-17	0.503*	0.505*
	(0.243)	(0.244)
South	0.086***	0.084***
	(0.016)	(0.016)
Sworn Officers / 1000 Residents (Ln)	0.238***	0.247***
	(0.025)	(0.025)
% Spending for Health, Education and	-0.001*	-0.001*
Welfare	(0.0004)	(0.0004)
Index Crime Rate Per 100,000	0.676***	0.663***
Residents in 1986 (Ln)	(0.022)	(0.023)
Social Disorganization Index	0.065***	0.083***
	(0.010)	(0.013)
Traditional Government Index		-0.009
		(0.009)
Social Disorganization*		-0.014
TG Index		(0.008)
Adjusted R^2	0.812	0.813

Note: N= 717. Numbers in Parentheses are standard errors. * $p < .05$, ** $p < .01$, *** $p < .001$

controlling for crime in 1986 and the other factors included in equation 1. Thus, whereas an overall measure of city expenditures was not related to crime in Table 2, a more targeted measure of city spending priorities is related to variation in overall city crime rates. Thus, it appears that cities that spend more on certain redistributive programs that benefit the poor can reap the benefits in terms of lower crime rates.

Equation 2 of Table 5.3 substitutes a continuous variable that is the sum of the number of traditional political system characteristics in a city, (TG index) to capture the cumulative effects of local political systems on crime, as well as an interaction between traditional government characteristics and the index of social disorganization. Although not significant at conventional significance levels, the coefficient for the interaction between the TG index and social disorganization is negative and approaches significance ($p = .092$). Thus, even controlling for prior crime rates, the relationship between social disorganization, traditional political systems and crime in Table 5.3 is consistent with the relationship found in Table 5.2. In other words, the effect of social disorganization on crime depends on the degree to which a city's political system can be characterized as reform or traditional. To illustrate, consider the effect on crime of a unit increase in social disorganization when the three dimensions discussed here are traditional versus when the city is entirely reform along these three dimensions.

Since the interaction term drops out of the prediction equation for cities with no traditional structures, for a one unit increase in the social disorganization index, one would expect an increase in the natural log of reported index crimes per 100,000 residents of .083 (the parameter estimate for the main effect of social disorganization). For a city with all the traditional structures, a unit increase in the social disorganization index is only expected to lead to a .041 (.083 + -.014 (3)) increase in the natural log of reported index offenses. Thus, the effect of social disorganization on reported index offenses in completely traditional cities is just less than half of its effect in completely reform cities. Once again it is important to note that, extant city-level crime research and social disorganization research do not predict that local political systems should account for any variation in crime rates. Taken together, the results of Tables 5.2 and 5.3 suggest that – individually and cumulatively – local political systems may be an important resource in the fight against crime, which has been overlooked in prior research. In the next section, I examine the role of another potential institutional resource – race of the mayor.

Race of Mayor

As discussed in Chapter 3, some prior research suggests that minority officials may be more likely to favor poor and minority interests (for example Karnig and Welch 1980), and some recent research suggests that this can have consequences for interracial crime (recall Jacobs and Wood, 1999). I argue that the race of the mayor may be thought of as an institutional resource that minority communities may be able to use to help further their interests in reducing crime. Therefore, this section examines whether the race of the mayor has any effect on crime rates. Table 5.4 presents the results of WLS regression analyses predicting the natural log of reported index offenses per 100,000 residents for 605 cities with 25,0000 or more residents in 1991. Equation 1 includes the control variables included in prior analyses, as well as the index of structural indicators of social disorganization and the continuous variable tapping number of traditional political structures. The results are remarkably consistent with those reported in Tables 5.2 and 5.3. Equation 2 adds a categorical variable coded 1 if the mayor of a city is African American and 0 otherwise. This variable is significantly negatively related to crime ($p < .05$). Substantively, this means that controlling for prior crime, the local political system, social disorganization, and other factors included in the model, cities with African American mayors had lower crime rates.

In other analyses not reported here, I examined whether the race of city council members was associated with crime. To test for race of city council effects, I created a variable that measured the proportion of a city council that was black and a variable reflecting the ratio of black and city council members in relation to the proportion of a city that was black. This measure was similar to the measure used in Shihadeh and Flynn (1996). Consistent with Shihadeh and Flynn (1996), race of city council is not related to overall crime rates in 1981 or 1991 (race of mayor was only available for 1991). Similarly, I found no effect for variables measuring the proportion of city council that was nonwhite. It is possible that the differences in effects between the race of the mayor and racial composition of the city council have to do with the concentration of responsibility and control. It could be that the likelihood of race having an impact on crime rates is simply greater for mayors than councils because mayors have more power over criminal justice policies than individual city council members.

Table 5.4. WLS Regression of Crime Rates on Race of Mayor, Institutional Resources and Social Disorganization in 1991.

Variable	EQ.(1)	EQ. (2)
Constant	2.616***	2.608***
	(0.211)	(0.211)
Population (Ln)	0.033***	0.034***
	(0.009)	(0.009)
% Age 5-17	0.573*	0.592*
	(0.264)	(0.264)
South	0.088***	0.081***
	(0.017)	(0.018)
Sworn Officers / 1000 Residents (Ln)	0.248***	0.248***
	(0.027)	(0.027)
% Spending for Health, Education and	-0.001	-0.0008
Welfare	(0.0005)	(0.0005)
Index Crime Rate Per 100,000	0.641***	0.641***
Residents in 1986 (Ln)	(0.026)	(0.026)
Social Disorganization Index	0.088***	0.096***
	(0.014)	(0.015)
Traditional Government Index	-0.015	-0.018
	(0.010)	(0.010)
Social Disorganization*	-0.025*	-0.026**
TG Index	(0.010)	(0.010)
Black Mayor		-0.064*
		(0.030)
Adjusted R^2	0.809	0.810

Note: N= 605. Numbers in Parentheses are standard errors. *p < .05, ** p < .01, *** p < .001

In sum, even controlling for prior crime, it appears that institutional resources are related to crime rates in cities with 25,000 or more residents in 1991. Specifically, the race of the mayor and specific measures of city spending related to health, education, and welfare are significantly negatively related to crime rates. All of these effects are consistent with an institutional resource perspective, but one would not expect these findings from a pure social disorganization perspective. In addition, the effect of structural indicators of social disorganization on crime depend on whether the city has a mayor-council form of government and the number of traditional local political structures present in a city. The effect of social disorganization on crime rates was lower in mayor-council cities than council-manager and commission cities. In addition, as the number of traditional structures increased, the effect of structural indicators of social disorganization on crime rates decreased.

INSTITUTIONAL RESOURCES AND CRIME IN 1981

In this section, I discuss the results of supplementary analyses performed on 1981 data. Similar to Table 5.1, Table 5.5 presents variable means by political structures for 1981. The pattern of results for 1981 data is similar to the pattern in 1991. Comparing columns A and B in Table 5.5, mayor/ council cities have lower crime rates than council-manager or commission cities in 1976 and 1981, despite having structural indicators of social disorganization that would suggest higher crime, such as higher unemployment, higher poverty, lower median incomes, more female-headed households, and lower education levels. This can be seen most clearly by the stark contrast in values of the social disorganization index created from these structural indicators of social disorganization (discussed earlier in the Chapter). Mayor-council cities have a social disorganization value of .270, whereas council-manager and commission cities have a mean value of -.116 (Recall that this variable is normed at Zero). Thus, from a pure social disorganization perspective the values would lead one to expect mayor/ council cities to have higher crime rates in 1981.

Table 5.5. Variable Means by City Political System Variables in 1981.

Political System	MC	CM	Partisan	Non-Part.	District	AL/Mixed
Column	A	B	C	D	E	F
N	264	487	206	545	99	652
Pop.	125154*	76889	117988	84734	86728	94938
Crime 81	7021.9*	7557.9	6908.2**	7543.9	7403.0	7364.4
Crime 76	6182.1*	6575.1	6136.4*	6550.6	6402.5	6442.2
SD Index	0.270***	-0.116	0.301***	-0.086	0.230*	-0.012
% Black	13.82**	10.22	14.78***	10.23	15.26*	10.91
Unemp.	7.30***	6.00	7.19***	6.18	6.94$^@$	6.39
% Poor	12.23*	11.1	12.28*	11.19	12.26	11.38
Med. Inc.	23236**	24684	23098*	24480	22772*	24304
Fem. HH	17.98***	15.54	18.37***	15.66	17.75*	16.2
% HS Grads	65.82***	72.14	65.99***	71.41	67.94$^@$	70.22
Age 5-17	19.5	19.28	19.23	19.42	19.23	19.39
City Exp/ Capita	549.3***	437.04	506.59$^@$	465.12	539.72*	466.89
PD/ 1000 Residents	1.97***	1.67	1.98***	1.7	1.87$^@$	1.76

Note: @p < .10 * p < .05, ** p < .01, *** p < .001.

The same holds true for partisan cities (see columns C and D of Table 5.5), which have 636 fewer crimes per 100,000 residents than non-partisan cities despite having much larger city populations and having worse structural indicators of social disorganization. In addition, consistent with 1991, mayor-council and partisan cities have higher city expenditures per capita than council-manager/ commission, and non-partisan governments, despite having lower median incomes in the city. As with the bivariate relationships seen in 1991, district cities do not have lower crime rates than mixed and at-large cities.

Comparing Crime in 1981 and 1991

Table 5.6 presents the results of three WLS regression equations predicting the natural log of the rate of reported index offenses per 100,000 city residents for 790 cities in 1981. Comparing 1991 (Table 5.2) and 1981 (Table 5.6), the patterns of relationships are very consistent for all the variables included. Only the natural log of the population, and percent of the population age 5-17 exhibit different patterns. In 1991 the population is significantly positively related to crime in all three equations, whereas the coefficient is negative and non-significant in all three equations for 1981. In addition, percent of the population age 5-17 is significantly positively related to crime in all three equations in 1991, whereas in 1981, youthful population is significantly *negatively* related to crime all three equations. One possibility for the differences between youthful population and crime in the two decades is that gang activity could have increased substantially over this period. Curry and Decker 1998 present evidence that this could be the case. It could also be that gangs became more involved in the drug trade over this period as well (For a discussion of drug sales by gangs see Chapter 4 of Curry and Decker, 1998.).

The categorical variable for cities in southern states is also significantly positively related to crime in all equations in both 1991 and 1981. In addition, the natural log of sworn officers per 1000 city residents, and the prior index crime rate per 100,000 residents (1986, 1976) are significantly positively related to crime in all equations in both 1991 and 1981. Contrary to the institutional resource perspective, overall city expenditures were not significantly related to crime in 1981 or 1991. Yet, recall that a measure city spending targeted to health and hospitals, education, and welfare was significantly negatively related to crime in 1991 (see Table 5.2). Unfortunately, this information was not available for 1981 so it cannot be determined whether a more specific measure of city spending would follow theoretical predictions. Future research should examine the relationship between various types of spending, political systems and crime.

Table 5.6. WLS Regression Results of Crime Rates on Social Disorganization and City Political Variables in 1981 (N=751).

Variable	EQ.(1)	EQ. (2)	EQ. (3)
Constant	1.954***	2.164***	2.399***
	(0.172)	(0.185)	(0.188)
Population (Ln)	-0.002	-0.004	0.006
	(0.005)	(0.005)	(0.005)
% Age 5-17	-0.704***	-0.763***	-0.616**
	(0.205)	(0.205)	(0.209)
South	0.083***	0.073***	0.058***
	(0.014)	(0.014)	(0.014)
Sworn Officers/ 1000	0.100***	0.081***	0.100***
Residents	(0.011)	(0.013)	(0.013)
Expenditures Per Capita	-0.029	-0.031	-0.031
	(0.022)	(0.022)	(0.021)
Index Crimes Per 100,000	0.789***	0.773***	0.729***
Residents in 1976 (Ln)	(0.021)	(0.021)	(0.022)
Social Disorganization Index		0.027**	0.053***
		(0.009)	(0.012)
Mayor/ Council			-0.060***
			(0.016)
Partisan			-0.036*
			(0.015)
District			0.034
			(0.019)
Social Disorganization			-0.029*
*Mayor/ Council			(0.014)
Adjusted R^2	0.768	0.770	0.780

Note: Numbers in Parentheses are standard errors. * p<.05, *p<.01, ***p<.001.

Equation 3 adds the local political system characteristics suggested by the institutional resource perspective. Consistent with Hypothesis 3, partisan cities had significantly (p < .05) lower crime rates in 1981. Contrary to Hypothesis 4, district cities were actually positively, although not significantly, associated with crime rates in 1981. This is a somewhat puzzling finding that warrants future research.

In addition, consistent with Hypothesis 5 and the results for 1991, the effect of structural indicators of social disorganization on crime was significantly smaller in mayor-council cities than in council-manager and commission cities. This suggests the robustness of the relationship between form of government, social disorganization and crime over time. In analyses not reported here, I also tested for the cumulative effect of traditional political system characteristics on crime in 1981, similar to the analyses reported in Table 5.3. Consistent with the results reported for 1991, the coefficient for the main effect of the traditional government index is negative and, an interaction term between the traditional government index and the index of social disorganization is negative and significant, suggesting that the effect of structural indicators of social disorganization on crime declines as the city's political system becomes more traditional. Therefore, the results suggest that the effects of the variables suggested by an institutional resource perspective are robust across the two time periods included in the study. In the next section, I discuss some analyses that further probe the robustness of the reported results.

SUPPLEMENTARY ANALYSES

In a series of sensitivity analyses I separated district, at-large and mixed cities, resulting in three-categories of electoral structures. Results were substantively similar to those reported above. In addition, I tested for the robustness of results depending on the operationalization of the dependent variable. Separate analyses that broke crime down into violent and property crime produced substantively similar results. Using a three-year average of the crime rate from 1991 to 1993 also produced similar results. I also ran the models reported in Table 5.2 using log of the crime rate in 1992 and the results were substantially similar. Thus, the effects relationship between city political systems and crime appear to be robust across model specifications. I also examined the possibility that the strength of the mayor might have an effect on the relationship between form of government and crime. As discussed in Chapter 3, American cities can have either a strong or weak mayor. Strong mayors generally have veto power over city council actions, significant control over city budget allocation, and appointment powers, whereas weak mayors generally do not (Engel, 1999; Svara, 1990). Therefore, I compared cities with strong mayors to cities with weak mayors in terms of veto power, budget setting and appointment powers. No significant differences appeared across cities in crime rates based on mayoral power.

Because the number of missing cases could affect results (see Berk, 1983 for a review), sample selection models were run to generate a hazard (the likelihood of exclusion from the sample) using: population, percent black, percent of population age 5-17, percent of owner occupied homes, percent poor, unemployment rate, percent of households headed by females, median income and percent of adults 25 or older who were high school graduates. Inclusion of the hazard in the WLS equations reported in Table 5.2 did not affect the pattern of results. Thus, it appears that the results reported in Table 5.2 are not affected by the cases missing from the sample.

INTERPRETING THE CURRENT RESULTS

Prior research has suggested that a number of social and economic factors are likely to be related to city-level crime rates. Urbanization, family disruption, ethnic heterogeneity, poverty, and residential stability are all expected to predict variation in city-level crime, according to a social disorganization perspective. These factors are all thought to limit the ability of communities to maintain social ties and informal social control. Despite the advances empirically and theoretically, until recently previous research has focused minimal attention on city politics as an explanation for crime. The institutional resource perspective described here suggests that variation in local political systems could play a key role in explaining the ability of communities to organize against crime.

Consistent with expectations, I found that the relationship between structural indicators of social disorganization and crime appears to be related to the form of government and the degree to which the political system is traditional or "reformed". Even controlling for prior crime, the effect of a structural index of social disorganization on crime was weaker in mayor-council cities and as the city political system had more traditional political system characteristics, which research suggests is associated with increased susceptibility to political pressure. This is a completely unexpected finding within a classical social disorganization framework but is consistent with the institutional resource perspective outlined in chapter 3. In addition, even controlling for prior crime, city expenditures on health, education and welfare, were significantly negatively related to crime in 1991. Also, as predicted, the race of the mayor had a significant negative effect on crime, even controlling for local political systems, structural indicators of social disorganization, and city expenditures. Taken together, the results presented here suggest that city political system variation may affect the ability of citizens to maintain public control and ultimately reduce crime.

CHAPTER 6:

Urban Politics and Police Strength

As discussed in Chapter 2, numerous studies have examined variation across cities in arrests, police expenditures and police employment (for example Jackson and Carroll, 1981; Jackson, 1986, 1989; Jacobs, 1979; Jacobs and Helms, 1997; Kent and Jacobs, 2004; Levitt, 1997; Nalla et al., 1997; Sever 2001, 2003). These studies have often been motivated by the differing predictions of rational choice and conflict perspectives. Rational choice perspectives argue that variation in police strength should be related mainly to changes in crime, whereas conflict perspectives suggest that police strength is driven primarily by the threat from economically or racially marginalized groups. With few exceptions (for example Sever, 2001; Stucky, 2001), previous studies of variation in police strength across cities have generally ignored variation in local political systems. This is somewhat surprising because city governments make decisions regarding the shape of local anti-crime policies. The institutional resource perspective, outlined in chapter 3, suggests that the structure of the city's political system, and its attendant susceptibility to political influence, is likely to be related to city-level variation in police strength. Specifically, the ability of citizens to influence the political process is expected to have an impact on the anti-crime policies pursued.

The goal of this chapter is to assess hypotheses 9 – 16, outlined in Chapter 3. The organization of the discussion is as follows: First, I discuss the results of WLS regression analyses, examining variation in police employment in relation to variables from rational choice and conflict perspectives, and variation in city political system characteristics. Following that, I discuss the effect of another source of city political variation—strength of mayor—on police employment.

103

Finally, I assess the robustness of the findings by comparing the results of WLS regression analyses of the number of sworn officers in 1981 and 1991.

WLS REGRESSION RESULTS: POLICE STRENGTH IN 1991

In this section, I assess the relationship between city politics and police strength in 1991. The dependent variable is the natural log of the number of sworn police officers per 1000 city residents in 1991. A thorough analysis of residuals for the equations reported in Table 6.1 suggested that the cities reported in Appendix C were outliers that affected parameter estimates and were therefore eliminated from further analyses.[1] It is important to note, however, that these outliers influenced point estimates only. The patterns of results reported here led to substantively similar conclusions whether the outlier cities were included or excluded. Residual analysis suggested that heteroskedasticity was problematic in these analyses as well. Therefore, analyses included a population weight. In general, once the population weight was included, log transformations were made where appropriate, and outliers were eliminated, residuals appear to be normally distributed. Therefore, the assumptions of least squares regression appear to be met.

Table 6.1 presents the results of four regression equations. Equation 1 includes several variables suggested by prior research such as population size, youthful population, cities in southern regional location, city expenditures per capita, and police expenditures per capita. Interestingly, the number of city residents is not consistently related to the number of sworn officers. Population does not have a significant effect on the natural log of the number of sworn officers in equation 1 and in equations 2, 3, and 4 the effect is significantly negative. In other words, net of the other factors in the model, larger cities have fewer police per 1000 residents rather than more. This is somewhat surprising because previous research has consistently linked crime rates to city population size. Consistent with some prior research (for example Liska et al., 1981), cities in southern states are associated with significantly higher police employment in 1991 ($p < .001$).

Table 6.1. WLS Regression of Natural Log of Sworn Officers per 1000 City Residents on City Politics in 1991 (N= 715).

Variable	EQ.(1)	EQ. (2)	EQ. (3)	EQ. (4)
Constant	-1.226^{***}	0.095	-0.395^{*}	-0.297
	(0.19)	(0.192)	(0.179)	(0.181)
Population (Ln)	-0.011	-0.024^{**}	-0.026^{**}	-0.023^{**}
	(0.010)	(0.009)	(0.008)	(0.008)
Southern Region	0.154^{***}	0.091^{***}	0.121^{***}	0.112^{***}
	(0.020)	(0.281)	(0.018)	(0.018)
% of Pop.	-1.041^{***}	-2.037^{***}	-1.492^{***}	-1.578^{***}
Age 5-17	(0.286)	(0.270)	(0.259)	(0.263)
Ln Crime in 1989	0.182^{***}	0.085^{***}	0.125^{***}	0.11^{***}
	(0.025)	(0.023)	(0.021)	(0.021)
Police Exp. Per	0.024^{***}	0.018^{***}	0.022^{***}	0.021^{***}
Capita	(0.002)	(0.002)	(0.002)	(0.002)
Expenditures Per	0.171^{***}	0.124^{***}	0.094^{***}	0.107^{***}
Capita	(0.019)	(0.017)	(0.016)	(0.016)
Percent Black (Ln)		0.064^{***}	0.050^{***}	0.051^{***}
		(0.007)	(0.006)	(0.007)
Unemployment		0.024^{***}	0.013^{*}	0.016^{***}
Rate		(0.003)	(0.003)	(0.003)
District			0.016	
			(0.017)	
Partisan			0.087^{***}	
			(0.020)	
Mayor/ Council			0.152^{***}	
			(0.016)	
Traditional				0.088^{***}
Government Index				(0.008)
Adjusted R^2	0.528	0.634	0.698	0.687

Note: Numbers in Parentheses are standard errors. * p < .05, ** p < .01, *** p < .001.

Somewhat surprisingly, cities with larger populations age 5-17 are significantly negatively associated with the number of sworn police officers, controlling for the other factors in the model.

As outlined in Chapter 2, the rational choice perspective suggests that police strength should be most consistently related to the reported crime rate. Previous research has not consistently supported this relationship (for example Greenberg and Kessler, 1982; Greenberg et al., 1985 Loftin and McDowall, 1982; Greenberg et al., 1985). Contrary to prior research, but consistent with Hypothesis 9, cities with higher reported index crime rates per 100,000 residents in 1989 were associated with significantly higher numbers of sworn police officers per 1000 residents in 1991 ($p < .001$) in all four equations reported in Table 6.1. Thus, it appears that the rational choice perspective is supported in the current study. In addition, cities that spent more per capita and spent more on police per capita had significantly more police officers per 1000 residents in all four equations in Table 6.1, which supports hypothesis 12. It appears that cities with greater resources devote them to hiring more police officers. Although consistent with a rational choice perspective, this finding is also consistent with the institutional resource perspective described in chapter 3.

The primary alternative to rational choice explanations of police strength in previous research has been the conflict tradition. From this perspective, one would expect variation in police employment to be related to the size of populations that threaten elite interests. Equation 2 adds two variables suggested by the conflict perspective. Both percent black and the unemployment rate are significantly positively related to variation in the number of sworn police officers in 1991, controlling for the other factors in the model. These two variables alone explain 12.7% of the variation in the number of sworn police officers. Thus, both hypotheses 10 and 11 are supported and suggest that the threat from both economic and racially marginalized populations drive police employment. This lends strong support for the conflict perspective and suggests that both classic Neo-Marxist and racial threat perspectives account for some variation in formal social control across cities. It is also interesting to note that the inclusion of unemployment and percent black reduce the magnitude of the effect of the southern region variable dramatically, although it remains significant. Thus, it appears that a substantial portion of reputed Southern punitiveness is actually explained by structural variables rather than cultural differences.

The institutional resource perspective suggests that the rational choice and conflict perspectives are limited because they ignore variation in local politics that is likely to affect police employment. Equation 3 includes the individual local political system variables suggested by the institutional resource perspective. Recall that these are categorical variables coded 1 if the traditional political system characteristic (may-council, district elections, and partisan elections) was present and 0 otherwise. It is hypothesized here that traditional political systems facilitate the hiring of more police because they make local officials more susceptible to political pressure. One straightforward way to appear to be doing something about crime is to put more police officers on the streets. Therefore, to the extent that city political structures facilitate the accountability of local city officials to the electorate, they are likely to increase the number of police employed.

The results in equation 3 are consistent with this line of reasoning. Consistent with hypotheses 13 and 14, both partisan elections and mayor/ council governments are significantly positively associated with police employment ($p < .001$), even controlling for the other factors in the model. Note that neither the rational choice perspective nor the conflict perspective would predict these results. Contrary to hypothesis 15, district cities are not significantly associated with greater police employment, independent of the other variables in equation 3. The traditional political system variables included in model 3 explain 5.2% of the variation in the number of sworn officers in 1991. To get a sense of the practical magnitude of these effects, one can exponentiate the parameter estimate associated with mayor-council and partisan cities. This provides the effect of having a mayor-council or partisan government on the number of sworn officers per capita versus council-manager / commission cities, or non-partisan cities. Mayor-council cities are expected to have nearly 1.2 more sworn officers per capita than council-manager or commission cities. This represents a major increase in sworn officers because the mean number of sworn officers in the entire sample is approximately 2 per 1000 residents. Likewise, one would expect partisan cities to have nearly 1.1 more officers per capita than non-partisan cities.

It is also interesting to note that the inclusion of the political system variables reduces the magnitude of the effect of the percent black and unemployment variables, although they remain significant. Thus, it is possible that some of the effect of these conflict variables may have been overestimated in prior studies that failed to control for local politics. Likewise, controlling for variation in city political systems reduces the magnitude of the effect of city expenditures per capita on the number of sworn officers, although it remains significant. Thus, consistent with Lyons (1978), it appears that some of the variation in city expenditures is related to local political systems, but this finding is not predicted by rational choice perspectives. Taken together, these results provide strong support for the institutional resource perspective.

Finally, Equation 4 substitutes the traditional government index variable described in Chapter 4. Recall that it is treated as a continuous variable, ranging from 0 to 3, depending on the number of traditional system characteristics present in a city. Consistent with the institutional resource perspective and hypothesis 16, police employment in 1991 increases as the number of traditional political system characteristics increases. Thus, whereas equation 3 captures the independent effect of these structures, equation 4 captures the combined effect of these structures. Clearly, the results in equations 3 and 4 suggest that the institutional resource perspective adds an important dimension to the explanation of variation in police employment across cities.

Strength of Mayor

As discussed in Chapter 3, the power of the mayor varies across cities (Engel, 1999; Svara, 1990). In strong-mayor cities, mayors have broad power over city budgets, veto power over city council resolutions, and broad powers of appointment. In weak mayor cities, mayors do not have budgetary control, veto power, or the power to make appointments. The institutional resource perspective suggests that the strength of the mayor is likely to have an impact on the kinds of policies that are implemented. If mayors face significant pressure from the citizenry, it stands to reason that mayors with broader power will have more of an impact on policies. Therefore, I expect that cities with strong mayors are likely to have higher police employment, all else being equal.

Table 6.2 presents the results of four WLS regression analyses of 595 cities with 25,000 or more residents in 1991.[2] As in Table 6.1, the dependent variable is the natural log of the number of sworn police officers per 1000 city residents. Equation 1 includes the control variables and the variables associated with the rational choice and conflict perspective and individual political system characteristics suggested by the institutional resource perspective. The effects of these variables are nearly identical to those reported in Table 6.1, suggesting that the additional 120 missing cases did not affect results. As in Table 6.1, and consistent with the institutional resource perspective, partisan and mayor-council cities had significantly higher sworn police officers per 1000 residents than non-partisan and council-manager or commission cities.

Equation 2 adds a categorical variable with a value of 1 if the city had a strong mayor format (indicated by control over the budget submitted to the city council).[3] Consistent with hypothesis 17, cities with strong mayors have significantly higher police employment than weak mayor cities ($p < .05$), even controlling for rational choice, conflict variables, and the individual political structural variables associated with the institutional resource perspective. Therefore, it appears that the power associated with the mayor's office has an independent positive effect on the number of sworn officers per 1000 residents. This suggests that political structure has an important effect on criminal justice outcomes that is not accounted for by the conflict or rational choice perspectives of formal social control. This effect has practical as well as theoretical significance. Exponentiating the strong mayor variable provides the increase in the number of sworn officers per 1000 residents one would expect in strong mayor cities versus weak mayor cities. Strong mayor cities are expected to have 1.05 more sworn police officers per 1000 residents than weak mayor cities. This represents nearly a standard deviation difference between cities based solely on the power of the executive.

Table 6.2. WLS Regression of Sworn Officers on Institutional Resources and Strength of Mayor in 1991, N=595

Variable	EQ. (1)	EQ. (2)	EQ. (3)
Constant	-0.499*	-0.449*	-0.316
	(0.201)	(0.201)	(0.199)
Population (Ln)	-0.028**	-0.030**	-0.028**
	(0.009)	(0.009)	(0.009)
Southern Region	0.121***	0.124***	0.122***
	(0.019)	(0.019)	(0.019)
% of Population Age 5-17	-1.472***	-1.473***	-1.515***
	(0.286)	(0.285)	(0.287)
Index Crime Rate Per 100,000	0.141***	0.135***	0.118***
Residents in 1989 (ln)	(0.024)	(0.024)	(0.024)
Police Expenditures Per	0.021***	0.022***	0.022***
Capita	(0.002)	(0.002)	(0.002)
Expenditures Per Capita	0.096***	0.092***	0.104***
	(0.017)	(0.017)	(0.017)
Percent Black (Ln)	0.051***	0.051***	0.052***
	(0.007)	(0.007)	(0.007)
Unemployment Rate	0.013***	0.014***	0.017***
	(0.003)	(0.004)	(0.003)
District	0.025	0.019	
	(0.020)	(0.020)	
Partisan	0.082***	0.085***	
	(0.022)	(0.022)	
Mayor/ Council	0.157***	0.125***	
	(0.018)	(0.022)	
Strong Mayor		0.052*	0.076***
		(0.022)	(0.020)
Traditional Government Index			0.071***
			(0.010)
Adjusted R^2	0.696	0.699	0.693

Note: Numbers in Parentheses are standard errors. * p < .05, ** p < .01, *** p < .001

Equation 3 substitutes the continuous traditional government index variable, which is the sum of the number of traditional political system characteristics (range 0 -3). Even controlling for the other variables in the model and regardless of whether the political system characteristics are specified individually or cumulatively, strong mayor cities have significantly higher police employment in 1991 (p < .001). Again, the strength of the mayor is not predicted to be important by either the conflict or rational choice perspective, but these results are consistent with the institutional resource perspective.

COMPARING POLICE EMPLOYMENT IN 1981 AND 1991

To assess the robustness of institutional resource on police employment, WLS regression analyses were performed on the natural log of sworn police officers in 1981. The equations reported in Table 6.3 are similar to models 2, 3 and 4 reported in Table 6.1. Comparing the results reported in Tables 6.1 and 6.3, the significance patterns are very consistent. There were only two differences in the patterns of results from 1981 to 1991. The first is that the natural log of city population exhibits weak positive effects on the natural log of police officers per 1000 residents in 1981 but moderately consistent negative effects in 1991. In addition, the effect of percent unemployed varied across the two periods studied. In 1981, percent unemployed exhibited significant positive effects on the number of sworn officers per 1000 residents, but when the individual local political system characteristics associated with the institutional resource perspective were included, the effect of unemployment dropped to non-significance. In 1991, this variable was consistently significantly positively related to police employment. The effects of the institutional resource variables are remarkably consistent in 1981 and 1991. Both partisanship and form of government have significant positive effects (p < .001) in 1981 and 1991. Contrary to expectations, district cities were not significantly associated with police employment in either 1981 or 1991. Traditional political system characteristics were also cumulatively significantly positively (p < .001) associated with the log of police employed per 1000 residents in both 1981 and 1991.

Table 6.3. WLS Regression of Natural Log of Sworn Officers per 1000 City Residents on City Political Systems in 1981 (N=790).

Variable	EQ. (1)	EQ. (2)	EQ. (3)
Constant	-0.565**	-0.294	-0.325@
	(0.188)	(0.179)	(0.178)
Population (Ln)	0.024**	0.006	0.007
	(0.009)	(0.009)	(0.009)
Southern Region	0.060***	0.071***	0.080***
	(0.017)	(0.016)	(0.016)
% of Population Age 5-17	-0.740***	-0.713***	-0.694***
	(0.215)	(0.200)	(0.202)
Index Crime Per 100,000	0.044***	0.035***	0.036***
Residents in 1979 (Ln)	(0.007)	(0.007)	(0.007)
Police Expenditures Per	0.006***	0.007***	0.007***
Capita	(0.0004)	(0.0004)	(0.0004)
Expenditures Per Capita	0.236***	0.188***	0.209***
	(0.025)	(0.024)	(0.024)
Percent Black (Ln)	0.055***	0.051***	0.050***
	(0.005)	(0.005)	(0.005)
Percent Unemployed	0.010***	0.004	0.005*
	(0.003)	(0.003)	(0.003)
District		-0.0005	
		(0.017)	
Partisan		0.082***	
		(0.015)	
Mayor/ Council		0.110***	
		(0.014)	
Traditional Government			0.073***
Index			(0.007)
Adjusted R^2	0.642	0.693	0.685

Note: Numbers in Parentheses are standard errors. * p < .05, ** p < .01, *** p < .001

SUPPLEMENTARY ANALYSES

In addition to comparing 1981 and 1991, I ran a number of supplemental analyses to assess the robustness of results. First, results reported in Table 6.1 are unaffected by whether or not the dependent variable is log transformed. In addition, analyses that included the outlier cities noted in Appendix C produce substantively similar results to those reported in Table 6.1. Analyses excluding cases where values were substituted for the district and partisan variables also produced substantively similar results.

Poverty is another indicator that has been used to capture economically marginalized populations in prior research. Including poverty and unemployment in the model produced multicollinearity, however. Alternative models that substituted percent poor for unemployment produced identical results.

One could also think of these issues in terms of the social disorganization perspective discussed in Chapter 4. In fact, the index of structural of indicators of social disorganization does have a significant positive effect on the number of sworn police per 1000 residents. Unfortunately, including the index of social disorganization does not allow me to assess the independent effects of two of its components-percent black and unemployment, which are prominent constructs in the conflict tradition that have been assessed in previous crime control research. Therefore, to enhance the ability to compare with prior police strength research, this chapter reports analyses with percent unemployed and percent black rather than the social disorganization index.

Because the number of missing cases could affect results (see Berk, 1983 for a review), sample selection models were run to generate a hazard, which is the likelihood of exclusion from the sample, using: population, percent black, percent of population age 5-17, percent of owner occupied homes, percent poor, unemployment rate, percent of households headed by females, median income and percent of adults 25 or older who were high school graduates. Inclusion of the hazard in the WLS equations reported in Table 6.1 did not affect the pattern of results. Thus, it appears that the results reported in Table 6.1 are robust across model specifications and not affected by the number of missing cases.

INTERPRETING THE CURRENT RESULTS

Prior research has suggested that a number of social and economic factors are likely to be related to changes in police employment. Most previous research has relied on either the rational choice or conflict perspectives to explain variation in police employment. Rational choice perspectives suggest that police employment is likely to be related to crime. Conflict perspectives, on the other hand, suggest that police employment should be related to the threat from economically or racially marginalized groups, but, as noted above, neither of these perspectives pay significant attention to the role of local politics. The institutional resource perspective outlined in Chapter 3 suggests some reasons why local politics might affect police strength.

Both rational choice and conflict perspectives receive support in the current study. Crime, unemployment and racial composition of the city were all significantly related to the natural log of the number of sworn police officers per 1000 residents in 1991. The results presented in this chapter suggest that variation in political systems is an important but previously overlooked factor in formal social control efforts by the state. Both partisan cities and cities with mayor/ council governments had significantly higher numbers of sworn officers per 1000 residents in 1981 and 1991. In addition, as the number of traditional political system characteristics increased, the number of sworn officers per 1000 residents increased. The strength of the mayor was also significantly associated with variation in the number of sworn officers per 1000 residents in 1991. Contrary to expectations, however, district cities were not significantly associated with overall police employment. In sum, it appears that institutional resources are an important factor that has been overlooked, in prior research that has examined variation in police strength across cities. To the extent that cities have varying levels of institutional resources for pressuring city officials, they also appear to have different size police forces.

Notes

1. For a discussion of the criteria used to eliminate influential cases see Appendix B.
2. The smaller number of cities in the models reported here reflects missing data in the 1991 FOG survey on the strong mayor variable.
3. Other analyses, substituting appointment power or veto power of the mayor, produced substantively similar results.

CHAPTER 7:

City Politics and Criminal Justice

Until recently, city politics has received minimal attention in most criminal justice research. Recent studies of both crime and policing have begun to address the role of politics. Yet, to date none has offered a consistent theoretical account of how and why politics, crime and policing should be related. The purpose of this book has been to begin to generate a theoretical understanding of how city politics and criminal justice are related. To do this, I draw on Hicks and Misra's (1993) political resource theory, which suggests that public policy outcomes will depend on the interests of groups involved and resources available to them as they pursue these interests. According to political resource theory, the structure of the political system is likely to be an important factor to consider in determining public policies. The urban politics research discussed in chapter 3 suggests that variation in city political systems resulting from progressive era reforms has consequences for the political representation of poor and minority groups and public policy. Using political resource theory as a blueprint, I synthesized the urban politics research to begin to develop an institutional resource perspective on crime and police strength. In the next section, I discuss the implications of this perspective and the current research for studies of crime.

INSTITUTIONAL RESOURCES AND CRIME

Perhaps the key macro-social question for criminologists is why crime rates are higher in some places than others. This has led to a major research effort to explain variation in crime rates across cities. Many of these studies rely either explicitly or implicitly on social disorganization theory. Consistent with social disorganization theory, studies have generally found that cities with higher social disorganization (poverty, family disruption and residential mobility) have higher crime rates. Yet, from a theoretical standpoint, critics have justly criticized social disorganization theory for its nearly exclusive focus on internal community dynamics is limited. In response to this criticism, recent research has begun to consider the context surrounding a neighborhood. Beginning with Bursik and Grasmick's (1993) discussion of levels of control, studies have begun to consider informal social control within the community as well as the relationship of the neighborhood with the larger context, particularly the city government in providing police services, in generating social control. To date, however, studies have not generally considered the possibility that variation in local political systems across cities might affect the ability of neighborhoods to procure services from the city government to help organize themselves against crime. One exception to this is Stucky (2003), who finds that city political system variation is associated with variation violent crime rates and that the effect of disadvantage on violent crime depends on the nature of the city's political system. To date, however, no studies have attempted to develop a theoretical account for how and why crime and city politics should be related.

The institutional resource perspective developed here suggests that variation in political systems across cities affects the likelihood that citizen groups will be able to make their voices heard in the city government. Research shows that certain political systems are more open to political pressure. Traditional governments – those with an elected mayor, partisan elections, and district-based city councils—seem to be more open to political influence than 'reformed' governments. Research shows that the level of agreement between citizens and elites is greater in cities with traditional political systems. Research also shows that public policy outcomes vary across city political systems. Of course, this is not surprising. The stated goal of reform was to reduce the influence of interest groups on government. It appears to have worked. Unfortunately, reformers may have thrown out the baby with the bathwater.

Consistent with expectations, the current study found that traditional city political systems are associated with lower crime rates in both 1980 and 1990 and that the more traditional the city is the weaker the link between social disorganization and crime. It appears that the insulation of reformed governments from public pressure may limit the ability of poor and minority groups to garner important resources to organize against crime. Recent research on public control suggests that this is an important element in reducing crime in neighborhoods. If neighborhoods require resources from the city government to organize themselves against crime, it seems reasonable that city governments which have more open channels of communication with citizens will be more likely to hear neighborhood concerns and provide needed resources to support community organization.

This study also has implications for social disorganization research. Recent systemic social disorganization research has focused on the link between public control and crime. This research suggests that the ability of neighborhoods to secure external resources through ties with the local government and police will affect neighborhood crime rates. To date, however, studies of public control have almost exclusively focused on how public control affects the neighborhood, and assumed that the target of neighborhood efforts to secure resources is essentially a constant. The urban politics research discussed above suggests that this is not the case. Some cities are likely to be more open to neighborhood efforts to reach out than others. Thus, future research needs to consider the patterned variation in local political systems that is likely to facilitate or inhibit neighborhood attempts to secure resources.

Recent ecological research has also focused on parochial levels of control. Sampson and his colleagues (Morenoff et al., 2001; Sampson et al., 1997; Sampson and Raudenbush, 1997, 1999) suggest that collective efficacy is a necessary element of neighborhood social control and mediates the degree to which disadvantage and crime are related. Sampson and Raudenbush (1997) define collective efficacy as social cohesion of neighbors combined with a willingness to intervene on behalf of the common good. Thus, informal social control is obtained, in part, by the willingness of neighbors to intervene. Yet, studies have not generally considered the links between political systems and collective efficacy. Recent studies suggest that informal control and city politics are linked. For instance, research shows that district city council elections (Bledsoe, 1986) and having a black mayor (Bobo and Gilliam, 1990) are associated with higher *political* efficacy for blacks. In addition, Marschall (2004) finds that people with higher political efficacy are more likely to become involved in crime watch groups and attend school board meetings. Similarly, recall that non-partisan systems depress voter turnout. Thus, if political systems affect the likelihood that people will feel it is worthwhile to get involved, then it seems reasonable that this willingness to get involved will have implications for collective efficacy. Thus, future research should examine the links between political systems and collective efficacy.

Recent research has begun to suggest that the lines between private, parochial and public control may be blurring (or blurrier than we first thought). Carr (2003) argues that the distinction between private, parochial and public in social disorganization is probably false. He suggests that traditional private and parochial spheres have given way to a "new parochialism" which is a combination of parochial and public control. His research suggests that parochialism in terms of private citizens intervening with other people as a form of social control doesn't happen as much as it used to. Instead, private citizens become involved in social control by invoking elements of formal social control such as the police or city government. This suggests that research needs to figure out how receptive the local government is likely to be to such efforts. In other words, if social control involves a partnership between citizens and the government, it seems we must consider how political systems influence that partnership. Clearly, Bursik and Grasmick's (1993) focus on public controls warrants further attention in studies that assess variation in crime rates across cities. This study is one attempt to clarify the elements of city government that are likely to affect neighborhood efforts to maintain public control.

Recent research has also considered the link between land use and crime (for example Holloway and McNulty; Wilcox, et al., 2004), consistent with Shaw and Mckay's original social disorganization model based on concentric zones. For instance, Wilcox et al., (2004) find that whether the land use is business or resident centered affects burglary and community violence. Similarly, Holloway and McNulty (2003) argue that the effects of public housing on violent crime will depend on the characteristics of the public housing and the geographic/ demographic characteristics of the neighborhoods in which housing units are placed. They find that the effects of public housing on violent crime in Atlanta vary considerably by the type and the context of surrounding neighborhoods. Research suggests that city political systems affect land use (for example Feiock, 2004). The interesting question is whether city political systems affect land use in ways that affect crime. Future research should examine the links between city politics, land use and crime.

The results of the current study also have implications for institutional anomie theory, which suggests that political institutions will mediate the effect of the economy on crime. Consistent with this focus on the interrelationship of economics, politics and crime, several studies have considered how social support and crime are related. For instance, Savolainen (2000) finds that the strength of the welfare state affects homicide rates cross-nationally. Similarly, Pratt and Godsey (2002, 2003) show a link between social support and homicide. In the current study city spending on health, education and welfare was associated with lower crime. In addition, it is interesting to note that mayor-council and partisan cities spent significantly greater proportions of their budgets on public health, education, and welfare. This is consistent with other recent research on the relationship between social support and crime. Clearly, it seems that when it comes to crime—you get what you pay for. Thus, future institutional anomie research needs to clarify which dimensions of politics affect crime, and to incorporate variation in city politics.

INSTITUTIONAL RESOURCES AND POLICE STRENGTH

Another key enterprise in criminological research is the explanation of variation across cities in formal social control efforts. Previous studies have generally relied on rational choice, conflict or organizational perspectives to explain variation in crime control across cities. Like city-level explanations of crime rates, city-level explanations of police strength have generally paid limited attention to local politics. Theorists seem to assume, in the case of rational choice theories, that public policies are the result of a perfect aggregation of individual interests, or, in the case of conflict theorists, that conventional politics will be ineffective in garnering important resources for the poor or racial minorities, leaving no middle ground to be explained. Or, in the case of organizational perspectives, police staffing levels are thought to be predominantly internally determined.

The institutional resource perspective developed here, on the other hand, suggests that variation in police strength across cities is likely to be related to local political systems. I hypothesized that variation in local political systems, which affects the susceptibility of the city government to political influence, could also affect local anti-crime policies. I suggested that – individually and cumulatively – traditional political system characteristics such as mayor-council forms of government, partisan elections, and district-based elections would be likely to make cities more responsive to citizen calls for more police, all else being equal. Consistent with the institutional resource perspective, in 1981 and 1991, cities with mayor-council and partisan governments had significantly larger numbers of sworn officers, relative to the population size, and police forces got relatively larger as the number of traditional political system characteristics increased.

In addition to the effects of broad differences in form of government, based on the institutional resource perspective I argued that more subtle differences across city governments could be related to differences in police employment. Consistent with expectations, strong mayor cities had more sworn officers, even net of other political system factors. Thus, the level of concentration of power in the mayor's office appears to have consequences for the kinds of anti-crime policies that are pursued.

Clearly the results of the current study suggest that previous explanations of variation in formal social control across cities have been too limited. The current results provide support for both rational choice and conflict perspectives, but variation in local institutional resources also affects formal social control. Thus, it appears that the rational choice assumption that public policies are a perfect aggregation of citizen preferences and the conflict assumption that institutional politics will be ineffective are incorrect. In addition, organizational perspectives which focus mainly on factors internal to the police agency appear to be limited as well. The reality appears to be that city political systems vary in ways that affect police staffing levels. Thus, the current study suggests that explanations of formal social control need to be reconsidered in favor of a more nuanced theory which accounts for how city political systems affect policing. Apparently, Wilson (1968) was onto something, although it appears that his account should have focused more on political structure than political culture. The institutional resource perspective developed here is a first step toward that end.

LIMITATIONS AND DIRECTIONS FOR FUTURE RESEARCH

The current study has a number of limitations to bear in mind. First, urban politics research does not predict stark contrasts in public policy outcomes based on variation in political systems. For example, studies have shown that differences in spending between traditional and reformed governments are limited to certain types of spending. Yet, it appears that these differences may be enough to matter for crime. Recall that Velez (2001) found that even small increases in resources to poor communities reduced victimization rates. It may be precisely these small differences across governments which make a difference in the resources necessary to reduce crime in very resource-starved areas.

Second, it is important to note that the measures of politics used here are relatively crude. The major argument here is that some cities are more open to political pressure than others. Yet, the study includes no direct measures of political responsiveness. In the future, direct measures of city government responsiveness and its effect on crime should be collected. In addition, community block grant data or other city programs might clarify the specific mechanisms by which city political systems affect crime. If city politics matters for crime and policing because of its influence on public policy, a fully specified theoretical account requires both the structures and the outputs of the city government.

Another limitation of the current research is the inability to directly assess the level of community organization and how it relates to political variation within cities. City-level data such as that used in the current study cannot assess variation in internal community dynamics across neighborhoods. Thus, it is possible that city political systems do not affect all neighborhoods in the same way. If only certain neighborhoods benefit from traditional political systems, then the results found at the city-level could be misleading. In addition, the hypothesized relationships between city political systems and crime imply that there is an intervening effect on local community organization. These intervening mechanisms cannot be directly assessed using city-level data. This is similar to the problem faced in studies that compare social disorganization across cities. The intervening informal social control mechanisms cannot be assessed directly with city-level data. Therefore, studies include structural indicators of social disorganization. Thus, one important step in future research is to find ways to measure community organization more directly in order to assess how local political systems affect community organization and ultimately crime. The recent development of hierarchical models may facilitate the modeling of these complex processes.

Another important limitation of the current project is the age of the data. Because it relies heavily on decennial census data, at the time of data collection, the latest year that information was available for many of the variables in the analysis was 1990. The recent release of 2000 census data makes it possible to update the study. In addition, because data from 1980, 1990, and 2000 will be available, it will be possible to examine relationships over time. Therefore, one goal of future research is to collect 2000 census data to provide three waves of data on cities.

The current data also did not allow for the examination of two explanations often discussed in past research on variation in crime across cities. Previous studies have debated the relative importance of absolute and relative deprivation (for example Bailey, 1984 Blau and Blau, 1982; Messner, 1982). Land et al., (1990) suggest that from a practical standpoint, it may be difficult to tease out individual effects of inequality and poverty on crime because cities with one are very likely to have the other. In other words, poor cities are also likely to have large income inequality.

The current data also precluded examination of segregation. Segregation has been identified as a key predictor of crime in prior research (for example Krivo and Peterson, 2000; Peterson and Krivo, 1993; Shihadeh and Flynn, 1996). Based on the current results, it is quite possible that local political systems could affect the relationship between segregation and crime. Recall from the above discussion of electoral systems that district elections favor poor and minority representation over at-large elections. It is reasonable to expect that the effect of racial residential segregation on crime will vary by electoral structure. For instance, to the extent that there is residential segregation in a district-based electoral system, minorities should have less difficulty gaining physical representation on city councils. In addition minority communities should be able to have a more direct tie to the local government, even in the absence of direct minority representation, because re-election depends on satisfying the local constituency. Thus, it may be easier to garner important resources against crime and poverty. On the other hand, in at-large systems where representation is not geographically tied, segregation is likely to lead to much lower representation of minority interests. Thus, it is reasonable to expect that the effect of segregation on crime will depend on local political systems. Therefore, an important step in future research is to examine the interrelationship between segregation, local politics and crime.

Another important step in future research is to examine other aspects of formal social control. Although police employment is examined here, other studies have focused on variation in police expenditures across cities (for example Jackson, 1986, 1989; Jacobs and Helms, 1997; Sever, 2001, 2003). In addition, it is possible that institutional resources could affect other aspects of police departments. For instance, one could assess the impact of local politics on the proportion of police who are minorities. Research in political science has suggested that aspects of local politics can have an impact on the racial composition of police forces (Alozie, 1999). It would also be interesting to see if political systems affect the kinds of policies implemented in police departments. One might examine whether form of government affects police training requirements, professionalism of police, or confidence in local police.

Another prominent issue in policing research is the issue of community policing (for example Skogan and Hartnett, 1997). One recent study suggested that cities with elected mayors were more likely to apply for and receive federal grants for community policing officers (Choi, et al., 2002). The authors of that study suggest that this is because of the potential for credit claiming in election campaigns. Zhao (1996) argues that community pressure is often the driving force behind the adoption of community policing. If traditional governments are more susceptible to and attuned to public issue priorities, it seems reasonable to wonder whether they are more likely to adopt community policing. Likewise, if community policing requires a partnership with the community, it seems reasonable that traditional cities might be in a better position to develop or maintain the citizen-government relationship necessary to make it a success. Therefore, future research should examine whether city political systems affect the likelihood of adoption or success of community policing programs.

Another step in future research is to assess the *partisanship* of cities and of public officials. The current study examined predominantly the structures of city political systems. Yet, conventional wisdom suggests that the kinds of public policies pursued depend on the political and ideological leanings of those occupying public offices. This is perhaps nowhere truer than in the realm of criminal justice policy (see Caldeira and Cowart, 1980; Jacobs and Helms, 1996, 1997). Traditionally, the Republican party has been considered the law and order party (Jacobs and Helms, 1996). Therefore, it is reasonable to expect that the party in power in local government will affect the kinds of anti-crime policies that are pursued. Consistent with this reasoning, Jacobs and Helms (1997), in a national-level analysis of law-enforcement strength over time, found that the party in power nationally affected the number of police. Thus, an important step in future research is to examine the effects of party in power and the ideological preferences of the electorate on police employment and crime.

In addition to local variation in partisanship, it is plausible that there are differences across states in the kinds of policies that are pursued. Indeed, some political science research suggests that state-level political and ideological differences may have important consequences for the kinds of public policies pursued. For instance, Erikson, Wright and McIver (1993) argue that states are remarkably consistent in their policy responses along a liberal-conservative dimension. They develop a composite index of policy liberalism that encompasses nine policy arenas such as tax policies, criminal justice policies, education, and consumer protection. It seems reasonable to expect that cities in states with more liberal policies will have lower crime rates because the strategies of these governments are more likely to ameliorate social problems that arise. This is especially likely to be the case in light of the current findings that local spending on health and hospitals, education, and public welfare affected crime and that spending on them as a proportion of the total city budget varied by political structures. Therefore, one avenue of future research is to examine political and ideological variation across states to determine if this variation has an impact on local crime rates.

CONCLUSION

Studies of variation in crime and police strength across cities have been prominent research enterprises in criminology. Although each has identified important factors associated with variation in crime and police strength across cities, I argued that each was limited due to failure of each to address the role of city political system variation. The goal of the current research was to address these gaps. The study makes several contributions to criminology. First, it begins to develop an institutional resource perspective on crime and suggests specific ways in which local political systems and processes affect social disorganization and variation in crime rates across cities. Research on the history of progressive era reforms suggests that one of the underlying goals of reformers was to limit the political influence of poor, minority and immigrant groups. There appear to be lingering differences in how city governments respond to citizen pressure that appear to result in differences in crime rates.

In sum, the institutional resource perspective outlined here suggests that city political system variation could be important in determining city-level variation in crime. Governmental forms and electoral rules provide specific institutional resources that certain groups can use to further their interests. To the extent that local electoral rules and governmental forms enhance the likelihood of certain groups gaining political representation and facilitate gaining resources from city government, cities may have lower crime rates.

Second, it begins to develop an institutional resource perspective on crime control and suggests the value of exploring variation in crime control strategies across political contexts. It appears that cities vary in the size of their police forces based on more than crime and the number of minorities. Cities that are more susceptible to political pressure appear to be more likely to respond to calls for more police. This may be due to the credit claiming opportunities that come from putting "more cops on the streets".

Third, this study reverses the current trend in much crime research by focusing on more cities and all types of crime. Most recent research has begun to focus on homicide in large cities. Clearly homicide data is the most reliable, homicide is the most serious crime, and it is concentrated in large cities. Therefore, it is not surprising that many recent studies focus on homicide. Yet, we run the risk of becoming the criminology of homicide in large cities. Studies such as the current one that assess other kinds of crime in cities, both large and small, provide valuable counterpoints to the ever narrowing foci of recent research, which now breaks down homicide by race of the offender and the victim as well as type.

The importance of city political systems for crime and police strength in the current study also suggests the value of applying new theoretical approaches from research in other areas. The institutional resource perspective outlined here draws on other research literatures in political sociology and political science to expand beyond the theoretical focus of traditional social disorganization theory. It is surprising that so many criminal justice studies invoke the word politics without considering the concepts that are the bread and butter of political scientists.

Of course, political influence can be a two-edged sword. For instance, Feiock (2004) argues that the insulation of city managers from politics leads to more efficient land use policies. In addition, the susceptibility of local officials to political influence can lead to the kinds of corruption that led to the call for progressive era reforms in the first place. This is no small concern. Yet, on balance, it seems that for criminal justice outcomes more political systems are better than more reformed ones. The current study shows that traditional cities had more police and fewer crimes.

References

Alford, Robert and Eugene Lee 1968. Voting Turnout in American Cities. *American Political Science Review* 62: 796-813.

Allan, James P. and Lyle Scruggs. 2004. Political Partisanship and Welfare State Reform in Advanced Industrial Societies. *American Journal of Political Science* 48: 496-512.

Alozie, Nicholas O. 2000. The Promise of Urban Democracy: Big-City Black Mayoral Service in the Early 1990s. *Urban Affairs Review* 35: 422-434.

Alozie, Nicholas O. 1999. Segregation and Black and Hispanic Group Outcomes: Policing in Large Cities. *American Politics Quarterly* 27: 354-75.

Alozie, Nicholas O., and Enrique J. Ramirez. 1999. "A Piece of the Pie" and More: Competition and Hispanic Employment on Urban Police Forces. *Urban Affairs Review* 34: 456-475.

Amenta, Edwin. 1998. *Bold Relief: Institutional Politics and the Origins of Modern American Social Policy*. Princeton, NJ: Princeton University Press.

Amenta, Edwin and Bruce Carruthers. 1988. The Formative Years of U.S. Social Spending Policies. *American Sociological Review* 53: 661-78.

Amenta, Edwin and Drew Halfmann. 2000. Wage Wars: Institutional Politics, WPA Wages, and the Struggle for U.S. Social Policy. *American Sociological Review* 67: 506-528.

Bailey, William C. 1984. Poverty, Inequality, and City Homicide Rates: Some Not So Unexpected Findings. *Criminology* 22: 531-50.

Banfield, Edward and James Q. Wilson 1963. *City Politics*. New York: Vintage Books.

Barrilleaux, Charles. 1997. A Test of the Independent Influences of Electoral Competition and Party Strength in a Model of State Policy-Making. *American Journal of Political Science* 41: 1462-66.

Barrilleaux, Charles, Thomas Holbrook, and Laura Langer. 2002. Electoral Competition, Legislative Balance, and American State Welfare Policy. *American Journal of Political Science* 46: 415-427.

Behr, Joshua G. 2000. Black and Female Municipal Employment: A Substantive Benefit of Minority Political Incorporation? *Journal of Urban Affairs* 22: 243-264.

Bellair, Paul E. 1997. Social Interaction and Community Crime: Examining the Importance of Neighbor Networks. *Criminology* 35: 677-703.

Belsley, David A., Edwin Kuh and Roy Welsch. 1980. *Regression Diagnostics: Identifying Influential Cases and Sources of Collinearity*. New York: Wiley.

Berk, Richard A. 1983. An Introduction to Sample Selection Bias in Sociological Data. *American Sociological Review* 48: 386-398.

Black, Donald J. 1976. *The Behavior of Law*. New York: Academic Press.

Blalock, Hubert. 1967. *Toward a Theory of Minority-Group Relations*. New York: John Wiley.

Blau, Judith and Peter Blau. 1982. The Cost of Inequality: Metropolitan Structure and Violent Crime. *American Sociological Review* 47: 114-29.

Bledsoe, Timothy. 1986. A Research Note on the Impact of District/ At-Large Elections on Black Political Efficacy. *Urban Affairs Quarterly* 22: 166-174.

Bledsoe, Timothy and Susan Welch. 1985. The Effect of Political Structures on the Socioeconomic Characteristics of Urban City Council Members. *American Politics Quarterly* 13: 467-483.

Block, Fred. 1987. *Revising State Theory. Essays in Politics and Postindustrialism.* Philadelphia, Pa: Temple University Press.

Blumstein, Alfred, Jacqueline Cohen, and Richard Rosenfeld. 1992. The UCR-NCS Relationship Revisited: A Reply to Menard. *Criminology* 30: 115-123.

Blumstein, Alfred, Jacqueline Cohen, and Richard Rosenfeld. 1991. Trend and Deviation in Crime Rates: A Comparison of UCR and NCS Data for Burglary and Robbery. *Criminology* 29: 237-63.

Bobo, Lawrence and Franklin D. Gilliam. 1990. Race, Sociopolitical Participation, and Black Empowerment. *American Political Science Review* 84: 377-393.

Brandl, Steven G., Mitchell B. Chamlin, and James Frank 1995. Aggregation Bias and the Capacity for Formal Crime Control: The Determinants of Total and Disaggregated Police Force Size in Milwaukee, 1934-1987. *Justice Quarterly* 12: 543-562.

Bridges, Amy and Richard Kronick 1999. Writing the Rules to Win the Game: The Middle-Class Regimes of Municipal Reformers. *Urban Affairs Review* 34: 691-706.

Browning, Rufus, Dale Rogers Marshall and David H. Tabb. 1984. *Protest is not Enough: The Struggle of Blacks and Hispanics for Equality in Urban Politics.* Berkeley: University of California Press.

Bullock, Charles S. III and Susan A. MacManus 1993. Testing Assumptions of the Totality-of-the-Circumstances Test: An Analysis of the Impact of Structures on Black Descriptive Representation. *American Politics Quarterly* 21: 290-306.

Bursik, Robert. J. 1989. Political Decision-making and Ecological Models of Delinquency: Conflict and Consensus. In Steven F. Messner, Marvin D. Krohn, and Allen E. Liska (eds.), *Theoretical Integration in the Study of Deviance and Crime.* Albany: State University of New York Press.

Bursik Jr., Robert. J. 1988. Social Disorganization and Theories of Crime and Delinquency: Problems and Prospects. *Criminology* 26: 519 -551.

Bursik Jr., Robert J. and Harold G. Grasmick. 1993. *Neighborhoods and Crime: The Dimensions of Effective Community Control.* New York: Lexington Books.

Caldeira, Greg A. and Andrew T. Cowart. 1980. Budgets, Institutions and Change: Criminal Justice Policy in America. *American Journal of Political Science* 24: 413-38.

Campbell, David and Joe R. Feagin. 1975. Black Politics in the South: A Descriptive Analysis. *The Journal of Politics.* 37: 129-162.

Cauthen, Nancy K., and Edwin Amenta. 1996. Not for Widows Only: Institutional Politics and the Formative Years of Aid to Dependent Children. *American Sociological Review* 61: 427-448.

Carr, Patrick J. 2003. The New Parochialism: The Implications of the Beltway Case for Arguments Concerning Informal Social Control. *American Journal of Sociology* 108: 1249-1291.

Chambliss, William J., and Robert B. Seidman. 1982. *Law, Order, and Power.* Addison-Wesley.

Chamlin, Mitchell B. 1990. Determinants of Police Expenditures in Chicago, 1904-1958. *Sociological Quarterly* 31: 485-494.

Chamlin, Mitchell. 1989. A Macro Social Analysis of Change in Police Force Size, 1972-1982: Controlling for Static and Dynamic Influences. *The Sociological Quarterly* 30: 615-24.

Chamlin, Mitchell B., and John K. Cochran. 1995. Assessing Messner and Rosenfeld's Institutional Anomie Theory: A Partial Test. *Criminology* 33: 411-429

Chamlin, Mitchell B., and Robert H. Langworthy. 1996. The Police, Crime, and Economic Theory: A Replication and Extension. *American Journal of Criminal Justice* 20: 165-182.

Chandler, Timothy J., and Rafael Gely. 1995. Protective Service Unions, Political Activities, and Burgeoning Outcomes. *Journal of Public Administration Research and Theory* 3: 295-318.

Choi, Chi, Charles C. Turner, and Craig Volden. 2002. Means, Motive, and Opportunity: Politics, Community Needs, and Community Oriented Policing Services Grants. *American Political Research* 30: 423-455.

Clear, Todd R., Dina R. Rose, Elin Waring, and Kristen Scully. 2003. Coercive Mobility and Crime: A Preliminary Examination of Concentrated Incarceration and Social Disorganization. *Justice Quarterly* 20: 33-64.

Crank, John. P. 1990. The Influence of Environmental and Organizational Factors on Police Style in Urban and Rural Environments. *Journal of Research in Crime and Delinquency* 27: 166-189.

Curry, G. David, and Scott H. Decker. 1998. *Confronting Gangs: Crime and Community*. Los Angeles, CA: Roxbury Publishing Company.

Dawson, Richard E., and James A. Robinson. 1963. Inter-Party Competition, Economic Variables, and Welfare Policies in the American States. *Journal of Politics* 25: 265-89.

DeFronzo, James. 1997. Welfare and Homicide. *Journal of Research in Crime and Delinquency* 34: 395-406.

Dye, Thomas R. 1966. *Politics, Economics, and Public Policy in the American States.* Chicago, Ill: Rand McNally &Co.

Dye, Thomas R., and James Renick. 1981. Political Power and City Jobs: Determinants of Minority Employment. *Social Science Quarterly* 62: 475-86.

Eisinger, Peter K. 1982. Black Employment in Municipal Jobs. *American Political Science Review* 76: 380-92.

Eitle, David, Stewart J. D'Alessio, and Lisa Stolzenberg. 2002. Racial Threat and Social Control: A Test of the Political, Economic, and Threat of Black Crime Hypotheses. *Social Forces* 81: 557-576.

Engel, Michael. 1999. *State and Local Government: Fundamentals and Perspectives.* New York: Peter Lang Publishing.

Engstrom, Richard L. and Michael D. McDonald. 1993. 'Enhancing' Factors in At-Large Plurality and Majority Systems: A Reconsideration. *Electoral Studies* 12: 385-401.

Engstrom, Richard, and Michael McDonald. 1982. The Underrepresentation of Blacks on City Councils. *Journal of Politics* 44: 1088-1105.

Engstrom, Richard, and Michael McDonald. 1981. The Election of Blacks to City Councils. *American Political Science Review* 75: 344-55.

Erikson, Robert S., Gerald C. Wright, John P. McIver. 1993. *Statehouse Democracy: Public Opinion and Policy in the American States.* New York: Cambridge University Press.

Feiock, Richard C. 2004. Politics, Institutions and Local Land-use Regulation. *Urban Studies* 41: 363-375.

Feiock, Richard C., Moon-Gi Jeong, and Jaehoon Kim. 2003. Credible Commitment and Council-Manager Government: Implications for Policy Instrument Choices. *Public Administration Review* 63: 616-625.

Fording, Richard C. 2001. The Political Response to Black Insurgency: A Critical Test of Competing Theories of the State. *American Political Science Review* 95: 115-130.

Fox, Kenneth. 1977. *Better City Government: Innovation in American Urban Politics 1850-1927.* Philadelphia: Temple University Press.

Gastil, Raymond D. 1971. Homicide and a Regional Subculture of Violence. *American Sociological Review* 36: 412-27.

Glaser, James. M. 1996. *Race, Campaign Politics, and the Realignment in the South.* New Haven, CT: Yale University Press.

Gottfredson, Michael R. and Travis Hirschi. 1990. *A General Theory of Crime.* Stanford, CA: Stanford University Press.

Gove, Walter R., Michael Hughes, and Michael R. Geerken. 1985. Are Uniform Crime Reports a Valid Indicator of the Index Crimes? An Affirmative Answer with Minor Qualifications. *Criminology* 23: 451-510.

Granger, Clive W.J. 1969. Investigating Causal Relations by Econometric Models and Cross-spectral Methods. *Econometrica* 37: 424-38.

Greenberg, David F., and Ronald C. Kessler. 1982. The Effect of Arrests on Crime: A Multivariate Panel Analysis. *Social Forces* 60: 771-90.

Greenberg, David F., Ronald C. Kessler, and Colin Loftin. 1985. Social Inequality and Social Control. *The Journal of Criminal Law and Criminology* 76: 684-704.

Greenberg, David F., Ronald C. Kessler, and Charles H. Logan. 1979. A Panel Model of Crime Rates and Arrest Rates. *American Sociological Review* 44: 843-50

Griffith, Ernest S. 1974. *The Progressive Years and their Aftermath, 1900-1920.* New York: Praeger.

Guest, Avery M. 2000. The Mediate Community: The Nature of Local and Extralocal Ties Within the Metropolis. *Urban Affairs Review* 35: 603-627.

Hackney, S. 1969. Southern Violence. In *The History of Violence in America*, H. Graham and T. Gurr, eds. New York: Bantam Books.

Haeberle, Steven H. 1997. Exploring the Effects of Single-Member Districts on an Urban Political System: A Case Study of Birmingham, Alabama. *Urban Affairs Review* 33: 287-297.

Hajnal, Zoltan L. and Paul G. Lewis. 2003. Municipal Institutions and Voter Turnout in Local Elections. *Urban Affairs Review* 38: 645-668.

Hannon, Lance and James Defronzo. 1998. The Truly Disadvantaged, Public Assistance, and Crime. Social Problems 45: 383-392.

Hansen, Susan Blackall. 1975. Participation, Political Structure and Concurrence. *The American Political Science Review* 69: 1181-1199.

Hassell, Kimberly D., Jihong "Solomon" Zhao, and Edward R. Maguire. 2003. Structural Arrangements in Large Municipal Police Organizations. *Policing* 26: 231-250.

Helms, Ronald and David Jacobs. 2002. The Political Context of Sentencing: An Analysis of Community and Individual Determinants. *Social Forces* 81: 577-604.

Hicks, Alexander and Joya Misra. 1993. Political Resources and the Growth of Welfare in Affluent Capitalist Democracies, 1960-1982. *American Journal of Sociology* 99: 668-710.

Hofstadter, Richard. 1955. *The Age of Reform*. New York: Alfred A. Knopf.

Holbrook, Thomas M., and Emily Van Dunk. 1993. Electoral Competition in the American States. *American Political Science Review* 87: 955-62.

Holloway, Steven R., and Thomas L. McNulty. 2003. Contingent Urban Geographies of Violent Crime: Racial Segregation and the Impact of Public Housing in Atlanta. *Urban Geography* 24: 187-211.

Huber, Evelyne, Charles Ragin, and John D. Stevens. 1993. Social Democracy, Christian Democracy, Constitutional Structure, and the Welfare State. *American Journal of Sociology* 99: 711-49.

Huff, C. Ronald, and John M. Stahura. 1980. Police Employment and Suburban Crime. *Criminology* 17: 461-70.

Ingram, Paul and Hayagreeva Rao. 2004. Store Wars: The Enactment and Repeal of Anti-Chain-Store Legislation in America. *American Journal of Sociology* 110: 446-487.

Isaac, Larry and William R. Kelly. 1981. Racial Insurgency, the State, and Welfare Expansion: Local and National Level Evidence from the Postwar United States. *American Journal of Sociology* 86: 1348-1386.

Jackson, Pamela Irving. 1989. *Minority Group Threat, Crime, and Policing: Social Context and Social Control*. New York: Praeger.

Jackson, Pamela Irving. 1986. Black Visibility, City Size, and Social Control. *The Sociological Quarterly* 27: 185-203.

Jackson, Pamela Irving, and Leo Carroll. 1981. Race and the War on Crime: The Socio-Political Determinants of Municipal Police Expenditures in 90 Non-Southern U.S. Cities. *American Sociological Review* 46: 290-305.

Jacob, Herbert and Michael J. Rich. 1981. The Effects of the Police on Crime: A Second Look. *Law and Society Review* 15: 109-22.

Jacobs, David. 1979. Inequality and Police Strength: Conflict and Coercive Control in Metropolitan Areas. *American Sociological Review* 44: 913-24.

Jacobs, David and Jason T. Carmichael. 2002. Subordination and Violence against State Control Agents: Testing Political Explanations for Lethal Assaults Against the Police. *Social Forces* 80: 1223-1251.

Jacobs, David and Ronald Helms. 2001. Racial Politics and Redistribution: Isolating the Contingent Influence of Civil Rights, Riots, and Crime on Tax Progressivity. *Social Forces* 80: 91-121.

Jacobs, David and Ronald E. Helms. 1997. Testing Coercive Explanations for Order: The Determinants of Law Enforcement Strength Over Time. *Social Forces* 75: 1361-92.

Jacobs, David and Ronald E. Helms. 1996. Toward a Political Model of Incarceration: A Time-Series Examination of Multiple Explanations For Prison Admission Rates. *American Journal of Sociology* 102: 323-57.

Jacobs, David and Richard Kleban. 2003. Political Institutions, Minorities, and Punishment: A Pooled Cross-National Analysis of Imprisonment Rates. *Social Forces* 80: 725-755.

Jacobs, David and Robert M. O'Brien. 1998. The Determinants of Deadly Force: A Structural Analysis of Police Violence. *American Journal of Sociology* 103: 837-862.

Jacobs, David and Katherine Wood. 1999. Interracial Conflict and Interracial Homicide: Do Political and Economic Rivalries Explain White Killings of Blacks or Black Killings of Whites? *American Journal of Sociology* 105: 157-190.

Jensen, Gary F. and Maryaltani Karpos. 1993. Managing Rape: Exploratory research on the Behavior of Rape Statistics. *Criminology* 31: 363-385.

Jenson, Jane. 1990. Representations of Gender: Policies to Protect Women Workers and Infants in France and the United States before 1914. Pp.152-177 in *Women, the State, and Welfare*, edited by Linda Gordon. Madison, Wi: University of Wisconsin Press.

Jones, Clinton. 1976. The Impact of Electoral Systems on Black Representation. *Urban Affairs Quarterly* 11: 345-56.

Jones, E. Terrence. 1974. The Impact of Crime Rate Changes on Police Protection Expenditures in American Cities. *Criminology* 11: 516-24.

Kane, Robert J. 2003. Social Control in the Metropolis: A Community-Level Examination of the Minority Group-Threat Hypothesis. *Justice Quarterly.* 20: 265-295.

Karnig, Albert K. 1979. Black Resources and City Council Representation. *Journal of Politics* 41: 134-149

Karnig, Albert K. 1976. Black Representation on City Councils. *Urban Affairs Quarterly* 12: 233-242.

Karnig, Albert K. 1975. "Private-Regarding" Policy, Civil Rights Groups, and the Mediating Impact of Municipal Reforms. *American Journal of Political Science* 19: 91-106.

Karnig, Albert K., and Oliver Walter. 1983. Decline in Municipal Voter Turnout. *American Politics Quarterly* 11: 491-506.

Karnig, Albert K., and Oliver Walter. 1977. Municipal Elections: Registration, Incumbent Success and Voter Participation. In *Municipal Yearbook, 1977* Washington, D.C: International City Management Association.

Karnig, Albert K. and Susan Welch. 1982. Electoral Structure and Black Representation on City Councils. *Social Science Quarterly* 63: 99-114.

Karnig, Albert K. and Susan Welch. 1980. *Black Representation and Urban Policy.* Chicago, Ill: University of Chicago Press.

Karnig, Albert K., and Susan Welch. 1979. Sex and Ethnic Differences in Municipal Representation. *Social Science Quarterly* 60: 465-81.

Kelleher, Christine and David Lowery. 2004. Political Participation and Metropolitan Institutional Contexts. *Urban Affairs Review* 39: 720-757.

Kent, Stephanie L. and David Jacobs. 2004. Social Divisions and Coercive Control in Advanced Societies: Law Enforcement Strength in Eleven Nations from 1975-1994. *Social Problems.* 51: 343-361.

Kerr, Brinck, Will Miller, and Margaret Reid. 1998. Determinants of Female Employment Patterns in U.S. Cities: A Time-Series Analysis. *Urban Affairs Review* 33: 559-578.

Kerr, Brinck and Kenneth R. Mladenka 1994. Does Politics Matter? A Time-Series Analysis of Minority Employment Patterns. *American Journal of Political Science* 38: 918-943.

Key, V.O., Jr. 1949. *Southern Politics in State and Nation.* New York: Random House.

Kittel, Bernhard and Herbert Obinger. 2003. Political Parties, Institutions, and the Dynamics of Social Expenditure in Times of Austerity. *Journal of European Social Policy* 10: 20-45.

Knoke, David 1982. The Spread of Municipal Reform: Temporal, Spatial, and Social Dynamics. *American Journal of Sociology* 87: 1314-1339.

Koper, Christopher S., and Gretchen E. Moore 2001. A Survey-Based Assessment of Factors Causing Changes in Sworn Force Size: Examining the Perceptions of Police Pp. 27-40 in *Hiring and Retention Issues in Police Agencies: Readings on the Determinants of Police Strength, Hiring and Retention of Officers and the Federal Cops Program.* A Report to the National Institute of Justice by Christopher S. Koper, Edward R. Maguire, and Gretchen E. Moore.

Korpi, Walter. 1989. Power, Politics, and State Autonomy in the Development of Social Citizenship: Social Rights During Sickness in Eighteen OECD Countries Since 1930. *American Sociological Review* 54: 309-28.

Korpi, Walter and Joakim Palme. 2003. New Politics and Class Politics in the Context of Austerity and Globalization: Welfare State Regress in 18 Countries, 1975-95. *American Political Science Review* 97: 425-446.

Korpi, Walter and Joakim Palme. 1998. The Paradox of Redistribution and Strategies of Equality: Welfare State Institutions, Inequality, and Poverty in the Western Countries. *American Sociological Review* 63: 661-87.

Krivo, Lauren J., and Ruth D. Peterson. 2000. The Structural Context of Homicide: Accounting For Racial Differences in Process. *American Sociological Review* 65: 547-59.

Krivo, Lauren J., and Ruth D. Peterson. 1996. Extremely Disadvantaged Neighborhoods and Urban Crime. *Social Forces* 75: 619-50.

Kubrin, Charis E., and Ronald Weitzer. 2003. New Directions in Social Disorganization Theory. *Journal of Research in Crime and Delinquency* 40(4): 374-402.

LaFree, Gary D. 1998. Losing Legitimacy: *Street Crime and the Decline of Social Institutions in America.* Boulder, CO: Westview Press.

Land, Kenneth C., Patricia L. McCall, and Lawrence E. Cohen. 1990. Structural Covariates of Homicide rates: Are there any Invariances Across Time and Social Space? *American Journal of Sociology* 95: 922-63.

Langbein, Laura I., Philip Crewson and Charles Neil Brasher 1996. Rethinking Ward and At-Large Elections in Cities: Total Spending, the Number of Locations of Selected City Services and Policy Types. *Public Choice* 88: 275-293.

Langworthy, Robert H. 1986. *The Structure of Police Organizations.* New York: Praeger.

Langworthy, Robert H. 1985. Wilson's Theory of Police Behavior: A Replication of the Constraint Theory. *Justice Quarterly* 2: 89-98.

Lee, Matthew R. 2000. Concentrated Poverty, Race, and Homicide. *Sociological Quarterly* 41: 189-206.

Leicht, Kevin and J. Craig Jenkins. 1998. Political Resources and Direct State Intervention: The Adoption of Public Venture Capital Programs in the American States, 1974-1990. *Social Forces* 76: 1323-45.

Levitt, Steven D. 2002. Using Electoral Cycles in Police Hiring to Estimate the Effects of Police on Crime: Reply. *The American Economic Review* 92: 1244-1250.

Levitt, Steven D. 1998. The Relationship Between Crime Reporting and Police: Implications for the Use of Uniform Crime Reports. *Journal of Quantitative Criminology* 14: 61-81.

Levitt, Steven D. 1997. Using Electoral Cycles in Police Hiring to Estimate the Effect of Police on Crime. *American Economic Review* 87: 270 -90.

Liebert, Roland J. 1974. Municipal Functions, Structure, and Expenditures: A Reanalysis of Recent Research. *Social Science Quarterly* 54: 765-783.

Lineberry, Robert L., and Edmund P. Fowler 1967. Reformism and Public Policies in American Cities. *The American Political Science Review* 61: 701-716.

Liska, Allen E., and Paul E. Bellair. 1995. Violent Crime Rates and Racial Composition: Convergence Over Time. *American Journal of Sociology* 101: 578-610.

Liska, Allen E. and Mitchell Chamlin. 1984. Social Structure and Crime Control Among Macro-social Units. *American Journal of Sociology* 90: 383-95.

Liska, Allen E., Mitchell Chamlin, and Mark D. Reed. 1985. Testing the Economic Production and Conflict Models of Crime Control. *Social Forces* 64: 119-38.

Liska, Allen E., Joseph J. Lawrence, and Michael Benson. 1981. Perspectives on the Legal Order: The Capacity for Social Control. *American Journal of Sociology* 87: 413-26.

Liska, Allen E., Joseph J. Lawrence, and Andrew Sanchirico. 1982. Fear of Crime as a Social Fact. *Social Forces* 60: 760-770.

Liska, Allen E., John R. Logan, and Paul E. Bellair. 1998. Race and Violent Crime in the Suburbs. *American Sociological Review* 63: 27-38.

Loftin, Colin and Robert Hill. 1974. Regional Subculture of Violence: An Examination of the Gastil-Hackney Thesis. *American Sociological Review* 39: 714-24.

Loftin, Colin and David McDowall. 1982. The Police, Crime, and Economic Theory: An Assessment. *American Sociological Review* 47: 393-401.

Loftin, Colin and Robert Nash Parker. 1985. An Errors-In-Variable Model of the Effect of Poverty on Urban Homicide Rates. Criminology 23: 269-85.

Lowenkamp, Christopher T., Francis T. Cullen, and Travis C. Pratt. 2003. Replicating Sampson and Groves' Test of Social Disorganization Theory: Revisiting A Criminological Classic. *Journal of Research in Crime and Delinquency* 40: 351-373.

Lyons, William. 1978. Reform and Response in American Cities: Structure and Policy Reconsidered. *Social Science Quarterly* 59: 118-32.

Maguire, Edward R., and Craig D. Uchida. 2000. Measurement and Explanation in the Comparative Study of American Police Organizations, pp 491-557 in *Criminal Justice 2000*, Vol. 4.

Maguire, Kathleen and Ann L. Pastore, eds. 2004. *Sourcebook of Criminal Justice Statistics*. U.S. Department of Justice, Bureau of Justice Statistics. Washington, D.C.: USGPO.

Maguire, Kathleen and Ann L. Pastore, eds. 1998. *Sourcebook of Criminal Justice Statistics 1997*. U.S. Department of Justice, Bureau of Justice Statistics. Washington, D.C.: USGPO.

Marschall, Melissa J. 2004. Citizen Participation and the Neighborhood Context: A New Look at the Coproduction of Local Public Goods. *Political Research Quarterly* 57: 231-244.

Marvell, Thomas B., and Carlisle Moody. 1996. Specification Problems, Police Levels, and Crime Rates. Criminology 34:609-646.

Maume, Michael O. and Matthew R. Lee. 2003. Social Institutions and Violence: A Sub-National Test of Institutional Anomie Theory. *Criminology* 41: 1137-1172.

McCrary, Justin. 2002. Using Electoral Cycles in Police Hiring to Estimate the Effect of Police on Crime: Comment. *The American Economic Review* 92: 1236-1243.

McDowall, David, and Colin Loftin. 1992. Comparing the UCR and NCS over Time. *Criminology* 30: 125-132.

McDowall, David, and Colin Loftin. 1986. Fiscal Politics and the Police: Detroit, 1928-76. *Social Forces* 65: 162-176.

McNulty, Thomas L., and Steven R. Holloway. 2000. Race, Crime and Public Housing in Atlanta: Testing a Conditional Effect Hypothesis. *Social Forces* 79: 707-729.

Mehay, Stephen L., and Rodolfo Gonzalez. 1994. District Elections and the Power of Municipal Employee Unions. *Journal of Labor Research* 15: 387-402.

Menard, Scott. 1992. Residual Gains, Reliability, and the UCR-NCS Relationship: A Comment on Blumstein, Cohen, and Rosenfeld. *Criminology* 20: 105-113.

Messner, Steven F. 1983. Regional and Racial Effect on the Urban Homicide Rate: The Subculture of Violence Revisited. *American Journal of Sociology* 88: 997-1007.

Messner, Steven F. 1982. Poverty, Inequality, and the Urban Homicide Rate: Some Unexpected Findings. *Criminology* 20: 103-14.

Messner, Steven F., and Reid M. Golden. 1992. Racial Inequality and Racially Disaggregated Homicide Rates: An Assessment of Alternative Theoretical Explanations. *Criminology* 30: 421-45.

Messner, Steven F., and Richard Rosenfeld. 1997a. *Crime and the American Dream*, 2nd ed. Belmont, CA: Wadsworth.

Messner, Steven F., and Richard Rosenfeld. 1997b. Political Restraint of the Market and Levels of Criminal Homicide: A Cross-national Application of Institutional-Anomie Theory. *Social Forces* 75: 1393-1416.

Miethe, Terence D., Michael Hughes, and David McDowall. 1991. Social Change and Crime Rates: An Evaluation of Alternative Theoretical Approaches. *Social Forces* 70: 165-85.

Mladenka, Kenneth R. 1991. Public Employee Unions, Reformism, and Black Employment in 1200 American Cities. *Urban Affairs Quarterly* 26: 532-48.

Mladenka, Kenneth R. 1989. Barriers to Hispanic Employment Success in 1200 Cities. *Social Science Quarterly 70*: 391-407.

Mladenka, Kenneth R. 1989. Blacks and Hispanics in Urban Politics. *American Political Science Review* 83: 165-191.

Morenoff, Jeffrey D., Robert J. Sampson, and Stephan W. Raudenbush. 2001. Neighborhood Inequality, Collective Efficacy, and the Spatial Dynamics of Urban Violence. *Criminology* 39: 517-559.

Morgan, David R. and John P. Pelissero 1980. Urban Policy: Does Changing Structure Matter? *The American Political Science Review* 74: 999-1006.

Murton, T. 1976. *The Dilemma of Prison Reform*. New York: Holt, Rinehart, and Winston.

Nalla, Mahesh K., Michael J. Lynch, and Michael J. Lieber 1997. Determinants of Police Growth in Phoenix, 1950 – 1988. *Justice Quarterly* 14: 115-143.

Neter, John, Michael H. Kutner, Chistopher J. Nachtsheim, and William Wasserman. 1996. *Applied Linear Statistical Models*, 4th ed. Boston, MA: McGraw-Hill.

Nolan, James J. III. 2004. Establishing the Statistical Relationship Between Population Size and UCR Crime Rate: Its Impact and Implications. *Journal of Criminal Justice* 32: 547-555.

Nunn, Samuel. 1996. Urban Infrastructure Policies and Capital Spending in City Manager and Strong Mayor Cities. American Review of Public Administration. 26: 93-111.

O'Brien, Robert M. 2003. UCR Violent Crime Rates, 1958-2000: Recorded and Offender-Generated Trends. *Social Science Research* 32: 499-518.

O'Brien, Robert M., David Schichor and David L. Decker. 1980. An Empirical Comparison of the Validity of UCR and NCS Crime Rates. *Sociological Quarterly* 21: 391-401.

O'Connor, James. 1973. The Fiscal Crisis of the State. New York: St. Martins.

Orloff, Ann Shola and Theda Skocpol. 1984. Why Not Equal Protection? Explaining the Politics of Public Social Spending in Britain, 1900-1911, and the United States, 1880s -1920. *American Sociological Review* 49: 726-50.

Osgood, D. Wayne and Jeff M. Chambers. 2000. Social Disorganization Outside the Metropolis: An Analysis of Rural Youth Violence. *Criminology* 38: 81-116.

Ousey, Graham C. 1999. Homicide, Structural Factors, and the Racial Invariance Assumption. Criminology 37: 405-426.

Parker, Karen F. 2004. Industrial Shift, Polarized Labor Markets and Urban Violence: Modeling the Dynamics Between the Economic Transformation and Disaggregated Homicide. *Criminology* 42: 619-645.

Parker, Karen F. 2001. A Move Toward Specificity: Examining Urban Disadvantage and Race-and Relationship-Specific Homicide Rates. *Journal of Quantitative Criminology* 17: 89-110.

Parker, Karen F. and Tracy Johns. 2002. Urban Disadvantages and Types of Race-Specific Homicide: Assessing the Diversity in the Family Structures in the Urban Context. *Journal of Research in Crime and Delinquency* 39: 277-303.

Parker, Karen F., and Patricia L. McCall. 1999. Structural Conditions and Racial Homicide Patterns: A Look at the Multiple Disadvantages in Urban Areas. *Criminology* 37: 447-77.

Patterson, Samuel C., and Gregory A. Caldeira. 1984. The Etiology of Partisan Competition. *American Political Science Review* 78: 691-707.

Peterson, Ruth D., and Lauren J. Krivo. 1993. Racial Segregation and Homicide. *Social Forces* 71: 1001-26.

Peterson, Ruth D., Lauren Krivo and Mark A. Harris. 2000. Disadvantage and Neighborhood Violent Crime: Do Local Institutions Matter? *Journal of Research in Crime and Delinquency* 37: 31-63.

Piven, Frances Fox, and Richard A. Cloward. 1971. *Regulating the Poor: The Functions of Public Welfare*. New York: Vintage.

Pratt, Travis C. and Timothy W. Godsey. 2003. Social Support, Inequality, and Homicide: A Cross-National Test of an Integrated Theoretical Model. *Criminology* 41: 611-644.

Pratt, Travis C. and Timothy W. Godsey. 2002. Social Support and Homicide: A Cross-National Test of an Emerging Criminological Theory. *Journal of Criminal Justice* 30: 589-601.

Quadagno, Jill. 2000. Promoting Civil Rights through the Welfare State: How Medicare Integrated Southern Hospitals. *Social Problems* 47: 68-89.

Quinney, Richard. 1977. *Class, State, and Crime.* New York: Longman.

Rebellon, Cesar J. 2002. Reconsidering the Broken Homes/ Delinquency Relationship and Exploring Its Mediating Mechanism(s). *Criminology* 40: 103-136.

Reisig, Michael D. and Jeffery Michael Cancino. 2004. Incivilities in Nonmetropolitan Communities: The Effects of Structural Constraints, Social Conditions, and Crime. *Journal of Criminal Justice* 32: 15-29.

Robinson, T. and Thomas R. Dye .1978. Reformism and Black Representation on City Councils. *Social Science Quarterly* 59: 133-41.

Rogers, Mary F. 1974. Instrumental and Infra-Resources: The Bases of Power. *American Journal of Sociology* 79: 1418-33.

Rose, Dina R., and Todd R. Clear. 1998. Incarceration, Social Capital, and Crime: Implications for Social Disorganization Theory. *Criminology* 36: 441-79.

Rosenfeld, Richard, Steven F. Messner, and Eric Baumer. 2001. Social Capital and Homicide. *Social Forces* 80: 283-309.

Ruhil, Anirudh V. S. 2003. Structural Change and Fiscal Flows: A Framework for Analyzing the Effects of Urban Events. *Urban Affairs Review* 38: 396-419.

Salzstein, Grace Hall 1989. Black Mayors and Police Policies. *Journal of Politics* 51: 525-544.

Sampson, Robert J. 1988. Local Friendship Ties and Community Attachment in Mass Society: A Multilevel Systemic Model. *American Sociological Review* 53: 655-79.

Sampson, Robert J. 1987. Urban Black Violence: The Effect of Male Joblessness and Family Disruption. *American Journal of Sociology* 93: 348-82.

Sampson, Robert J. 1985. Race and Criminal Violence: A Demographically Disaggregated Analysis of Urban Homicide. *Crime and Delinquency* 31: 47-82.

Sampson, Robert J. and W. Byron Groves. 1989. Community Structure and Crime: Testing Social-Disorganization Theory. *American Journal of Sociology* 94: 774-802.

Sampson, Robert J., Jeffrey D. Morenoff and Felton Earls. 1999. Beyond Social Capital: Spatial Dynamics of Collective Efficacy for Children. *American Sociological Review* 64: 633-660.

Sampson, Robert J., and Stephen W. Raudenbush. 1999. Systemic Social Observation of Public Spaces: A New Look at Disorder in Urban Neighborhoods *American Journal of Sociology* 105: 603-651.

Sampson, Robert J., Stephen Raudenbush and Felton Earls. 1997. Neighborhoods and Violent Crime: A Multilevel Study of Collective Efficacy. *Science* 277: 918-924.

Sampson, Robert J., and William J. Wilson. 1995. Toward a Theory of Race, Crime, and Urban Inequality. In *Crime and Inequality*, John Hagan and Ruth Peterson, eds. Stanford, CA.; Stanford University Press

Santoro, Wayne A. 1995. Black Politics and Employment Policies: The Determinants of Local Government Affirmative Action. *Social Science Quarterly* 76: 795-806.

SAS Institute Inc. 1989. *SAS/STAT® User's Guide, Version 6, Fourth Edition, Volume 2.* Cary, NC: SAS Institute Inc.

Sass, Tim R. 2000. The Determinants of Hispanic Representation in Municipal Government. *Southern Economic Journal* 66: 609-630.

Sass, Tim R., and Stephen L. Mehay 1995. The Voting Rights Act, District Elections, and the Success of Black Candidates in Municipal Elections. *The Journal of Law and Economics.* 38: 367-392.

Sass, Tim R., and Bobby J. Pittmann, Jr. 2000. The Changing Impact of Electoral Structure on Black Representation in the South, 1970-1996. *Public Choice* 104: 369-388.

Sass, Tim R. and Jennifer L. Troyer. 1999. Affirmative Action, Political Representation, Unions, and Female Police Employment. *Journal of Labor Research* 20: 571-587.

Savolainen, Jukka. 2000. Inequality, Welfare State, and Homicide: Further Support for the Institutional Anomie Theory. *Criminology* 38: 1021-1043.

Scarrow, Howard A. 1999. The Impact of At-Large Elections: Vote Dilution or Choice Dilution. *Electoral Studies* 18: 557-567.

Sever, Brion. 2003. The Minority Population/ Police Strength Relationship: Exploring Past Research. *Criminal Justice Studies* 16: 153-171.

Sever, Brion. 2001. The Relationship Between Minority Populations and Police Force Strength: Expanding Our Knowledge. *Police Quarterly* 4: 28-68.

Sharp, Elaine B. 2002. Culture, Institutions, and Urban Officials' Responses to Morality Issues. *Political Research Quarterly* 55: 861-883.

Sharp, Elaine B. 1991. Institutional Manifestations of Accessibility and Urban Economic Development Policy. *The Western Political Quarterly* 44: 129-147.

Shaw, Clifford R. and Henry D. Mckay. 1972. *Juvenile Delinquency and Urban Areas*, Revised ed. Chicago, Ill: University of Chicago Press.

Sherman, Lawrence W. Fair and Effective Policing. Pp. 383-412 in *Crime: Public Policies for Crime Control*, Wilson, James Q., and Joan Petersilia, eds. Oakland, Ca: ICS Press.

Shihadeh, Edward S. and Wesley Shrum. 2004. Serious Crime in Urban Neighborhoods: Is There a Race Effect? *Sociological Spectrum* 24: 507-33.

Shihadeh, Edward S., and Nicole Flynn. 1996. Segregation and Crime: The Effects of Social Isolation on the Rates of Black Urban Violence. *Social Forces* 74: 325-52.

Shihadeh, Edward S. and Graham C. Ousey. 1998. Industrial Restructuring and Violence: The Link Between Entry-Level Jobs, Economic Deprivation, and Black and White Homicide. *Social Forces* 77: 185-206.

Shihadeh, Edward S. and Graham C. Ousey. 1996. Metropolitan Expansion and Black Social Dislocation: The Link Between Suburbanization and Center-City Crime. *Social Forces* 75: 649-66.

Shihadeh, Edward S. and Darrell J. Steffensmeier. 1994. Economic Inequality, Family Disruption, and Urban Black Violence: Cities as Units of Stratification and Social Control. *Social Forces* 73: 729-51.

Shumaker, Paul and Russell W. Getter 1983. Structural Sources of Unequal Responsiveness to Group Demands in American Cities. *The Western Political Quarterly* 36: 7-29.

Silver, Eric and Lisa L. Miller. 2004. Sources of Informal Social Control in Chicago Neighborhoods. *Criminology* 42: 551-583.

Skogan, Wesley G., and Susan M. Hartnett. 1997. *Community Policing, Chicago Style*. New York: Oxford University Press.

Slovak, Jeffrey S. 1986. *Styles of Urban Policing: Organization, Environment, and Police Styles in Selected American Cities.* New York University Press.

Smith, Kevin B. 2004. The Politics of Punishment: Evaluating Political Explanations of Incarceration Rates. *The Journal of Politics* 66: 925-938.

Smith, William R., Sharon Glave Frazee, and Elizabeth L. Davison. 2000. Furthering the Integration of Routine Activity and Social Disorganization Theories: Small Units of Analysis and the Study of Street Robbery as a Diffusion Process. *Criminology* 38: 489-523.

Soule, Sarah A. and Susan Olzak. 2004. When Do Movements Matter? The Politics of Contingency and the Equal Rights Amendment. *American Sociological Review* 69: 473-497.

Soule, Sarah A. and Nella Van Dyke. 1999. Black Church Arson in the United States, 1989-1996. *Ethnic and Racial Studies* 22: 724-742.

Steed, Robert P. 1997. Introduction: Changing Electoral and Party Politics in the South. Pp.1-8 in *Southern Parties and Elections*, Steed, Robert P., Laurence W. Moreland, and Tod A. Baker (eds.), Tuscaloosa, AL: University of Alabama Press.

Stolzenberg, Lisa, Stewart J. D'Alessio, and David Eitle. 2004. A Multilevel Test of Racial Threat Theory. *Criminology* 42: 673-698.

Strate, John, Harold Wolman, and Alan Melchior. 1993. Are Three Election-Driven Tax-and-Expenditure Cycles for Urban Governments? *Urban Affairs Quarterly* 28: 462-479.

Stucky, Thomas D. 2003. Local Politics and Violent Crime in U.S. Cities. *Criminology* 41: 1101-1136.

Stucky, Thomas D. 2001. *An Institutional Resources Perspective on Crime and Crime Control in U.S. Cities.* Unpublished Doctoral Dissertation Manuscript, University of Iowa, Iowa City, IA.

Sun, Ivan Y., Ruth A. Triplett, and Randy R. Gainey. 2004. Social Disorganization, Legitimacy or Local Institutions, and Neighborhood Crime: An Explanatory Study of Perceptions of the Police and Local Government. *Journal of Crime and Justice* 27: 33-60.

Svara, John. 1990. *Official Leadership in the City*. Oxford, UK: Oxford University Press.

Swimmer, Gene. 1974. The Relationship of Police and Crime: Some Methodological and Empirical Results. *Criminology* 12: 293-314.

Taylor, Ralph B. 1997. Social Order and Disorder of Street Blocks and Neighborhoods: Ecology, Microecology, and the Systemic Model of Social Disorganization. *Journal of Research in Crime and Delinquency* 34: 113-55.

Trejo, Stephen 1991. Public Sector Unions and Municipal Employment. *Industrial and Labor Relations Review* 45: 162-180.

Vedlitz, Arnold and Charles A. Johnson. 1982. Community Racial Segregation, Electoral Structure and Minority Representation. *Social Science Quarterly* 63: 729-736.

Velez, Maria B. 2001. The Role of Public Social Control in Urban Neighborhoods: A Multi-Level Analysis of Victimization Risk. *Criminology* 39: 837-863.

Triplett, Ruth A., Randy R. Gainey, and Ivan Y. Sun. 2003. Institutional Strength, Social Control, and Neighborhood Crime Rates. *Theoretical Criminology* 7: 439-467.

Turk, Austin. 1969. *Criminality and Legal Order*. Chicago, Ill: Rand McNally.

Urban Data Service. 1997. Municipal Form of Government-1996. Survey conducted by the International City Management Association, Washington, D.C.

Urban Data Service. 1992. Municipal Form of Government-1991. Survey conducted by the International City Management Association, Washington, D.C.

Urban Data Service. 1987. Municipal Form of Government-1986. Survey conducted by the International City Management Association, Washington, D.C.

Urban Data Service. 1982. Form of Government-1981. Survey conducted by the International City Management Association, Washington, D.C.

U.S. Department of Commerce. Bureau of the Census. 2000. *County and City Data Book* [United States], 1994 (computer file). Washington, D.C: US Dept. of Commerce, Bureau of the Census. Generated via University of Virginia website, <http://fisher.lib.virginia.edu/ccdb/city94.html 1994>; (02 August 2000).

U.S. Department of Commerce. Bureau of the Census. 1984. *County and City Data Book*, 1983 (computer file). Washington, D.C: US Dept. of Commerce, Bureau of the Census, 1984 (producer). Ann Arbor Mi: Inter-University Consortium for Political and Social Research, 1984 (distributor).

U.S. Department of Justice, Federal Bureau of Investigation. 2000a. *Uniform Crime Reporting Program Data: 1975-1997* [Offenses Known and Clearances by Arrest, various years] (Computer file). Compiled by the U.S. Dept. of Justice, Federal Bureau of Investigation. ICPSR ed. Ann Arbor, MI: Inter-university Consortium for Political and Social Research (producer and distributor), 2000.

U.S. Department of Justice, Federal Bureau of Investigation. 2000b. *Uniform Crime Reporting Data: 1975-1997* [Police Employee (LEOKA) Data, various years] (Computer file). Compiled by the U.S. Dept. of Justice, Federal Bureau of Investigation. ICPSR ed. Ann Arbor, MI: Inter-university Consortium for Political and Social Research (producer and distributor), 2000.

U.S. Department of Justice, Bureau of Justice Statistics. 1996. *Law Enforcement Management and Administrative Statistics (LEMAS) 1990*, (Computer file). Conducted by U.S. Dept. of Commerce, Bureau of the Census. ICPSR ed. Ann Arbor, MI: Inter-university Consortium for Political and Social Research (producer and distributor), 1996.

Van Dyke, Nella and Sarah A. Soule. 2002. Structural Social Change and the Mobilizing Effect of Threat: Explaining Levels of Patriot and Militia Organizing in the United States. *Social Problems* 49: 497-520.

Velez, Maria B., Lauren J. Krivo, and Ruth D. Peterson. 2003. Structural Inequality and Homicide: An Assessment of the Black-White Gap in Killings. *Criminology* 41: 645-672.

Wadsworth, Tim and Charis E. Kubrin. 2004. Structural Factors and Black Interracial Homicide: A New Examination of the Causal Process. *Criminology* 42: 647-672.

Warner, Barbara D. 2003. The Role of Attenuated Culture in Social Disorganization Theory. *Criminology* 41: 73-97.

Warner, Barbara D., and Glenn L. Pierce. 1993. Reexamining Social Disorganization Using Calls to the Police as a Measure of Crime. *Criminology* 31: 493-517.

Warner, Barbara D., and Pamela Wilcox Rountree. 1997. Local Social Ties in a Community and Crime Model: Questioning the Systemic Nature of Informal Control. *Social Problems* 44: 520-36.

Weir, Margaret and Theda Skocpol. 1985. State Structures and Keynesian Responses to the Great Depression in Sweden, Britain, and the United States. Pp. 107-68 *Bringing the State Back In*, edited by Peter Evans, Dietrich Rueschemeyer, and Theda Skocpol. New York: Cambridge University Press.

Welch, Susan. 1990. The Impact of At-Large Elections on the Representation of Blacks and Hispanics. *Journal of Politics* 52: 1050-75.

Welch, Susan and Timothy Bledsoe. 1988. *Urban Reform and Its Consequences*. Chicago, Ill: University of Chicago Press.

Welch, Susan and Timothy Bledsoe. 1986. The Partisan Consequences of Nonpartisan Elections and the Changing Nature of Urban Politics. *American Journal of Political Science* 30: 128-39.

Wells, Edward L., David N. Falcone, and Cara Rabe-Hemp. 2001. Community Characteristics and Policing Styles in Suburban Agencies. *Policing* 26: 566-590.

Wilcox, Pamela, Neil Quisenberry, Debra T. Cabrera, and Shayne Jones. 2004. Busy Places and Broken Windows? Toward Defining the Role of Physical Structure and Process in Community Crime Models. *Sociological Quarterly* 45: 185-207.

Wilensky, Harold. 1975. *The Welfare State and Equality: Structural and Ideological Roots of Public Expenditures*. Berkley, Ca: University of California Press.

Williams, Kirk R. 1984. Economic Sources of Homicide: Reestimating the Effects of Poverty and Inequality. *American Sociological Review* 49: 283-89.

Wilson, James Q. 1968. *Varieties of Police Behavior: The Management of Law and Order in Eight Communities*. Harvard University Press.

Wilson, James Q. and Barbara Boland. 1978. The Effect of Police on Crime. *Law and Society Review* 12: 367-90.

Wilson, William Julius. 1987. *The Truly Disadvantaged: The Inner City, the Underclass, and Public Policy*. University of Chicago Press.

Wolfgang, Marvin and Franco Ferracuti. 1967. *The Subculture of Violence*. London: Tavistock.

Wolman, Harold, John Strate and Alan Melchior. 1996. Does Changing Mayors Matter? *Journal of Politics* 58: 201-223.

Wong, Kenneth K. 1988. Economic Constraint and Political Choice in Urban Policymaking. *American Journal of Political Science* 32: 1-18.

Wood, Curtis. 2002. Voter Turnout in City Elections. *Urban Affairs Review* 38: 209-231.

Zax, Jeffrey S 1990. Election Methods and Black and Hispanic City Council Membership. *Social Science Quarterly* 71: 339-355.

Zhao, Jihong 1996. *Why Police Organizations Change: A Study of Community Oriented Policing.* Washington, DC: Police Executive Research Forum.

Appendix A

QUESTIONS USED TO CONSTRUCT LOCAL POLITICAL VARIABLES

Source: Form of Government surveys of cities with population 2500 or greater conducted in 1981 and 1991 (Urban Data Service, 1982, 1992).

Mayor/ Council

Coded 1 if mayor/council and 0 otherwise.

1981 Question 1: Please indicate which of the following best describes your current legal form of government.
1. Mayor/ Council
2. Council/ Manager
3. Commission
4. Town Meeting
5. Representative Town Meeting

1991 Question 1: Indicate your current form of government as defined by your charter, ordinance, or state law.
1. Mayor/ Council
2. Council/ Manager
3. Commission
4. Town Meeting
5. Representative Town Meeting

District v. At-large
1981-Coded 1 if district and 0 otherwise.

Question 16: What kind of electoral system does your municipality have?
1. At-Large
2. Elections by ward or district
3. Combination

1991-Coded 1 if 100% nominated and elected by districts and 0 otherwise.

Question 29: Indicate the number of council members selected by each of the following methods?
1. Nominated and elected at large
2. Nominated by ward or district and elected at large
3. Nominated by ward or district and elected by ward or district
4. Other
   a. Total council members listed in 1 – 4.

Partisan v. Non-partisan

Coded 1 if political party appears on ballot and 0 otherwise.

1981-Question 5: Does the political party affiliation of candidates appear on the ballot in a general election?
   1. Yes   2. No

1991-Question 21: Does the political party affiliation of candidates for board or council appear on the ballot in a local general election?
   1. No   2. Yes

Race of Mayor

1991-Question 10: What is the ethnic background of the current mayor?
1. American Indian
2. Hispanic
3. Asian or Pacific Islander
4. White, not of Hispanic Origin
5. Black, not of Hispanic Origin

Strength of Mayor

1991-Question 5: Who has the overall responsibility for developing the budget submitted to the council?
1. Mayor   2. CAO
3. Combination CAO and Mayor   4. Other

Considered strong mayor if answer to question 5 is 1.

Appendix B: Table 1. Correlation Matrix for Chapter 5 Models, N=717.

Variable	1	2	3	4	5	6	7	8	9	10	11	12	13	14
1. Ln Crime 91	1.0	**.36**	.06	**.36**	**.23**	**.43**	**.60**	.04	-.05	-.05	**.84**	-.03	-.03	**.21**[a]
2. Ln Pop 91		1.0	.07	**.10**	**.23**	.07	**.19**	.01	.01	-.05	**.37**	-.01	.06	**.16**[a]
3. % 5-17			1.0	-.00	-**.22**	-**.22**	-**.21**	**.11**	.02	-**.10**	.05	-.03	-**.13**	.06[a]
4. South				1.0	.01	**.26**	**.32**	.06	-**.12**	-.07	**.29**	-.06	.01	-.06[a]
5. Exp / Cap.					1.0	**.33**	**.17**	-.01	**.12**	**.08**	**.21**	**.09**	**.64**	**.15**[a]
6. Off./10³ Res.						1.0	**.41**	**.09**	**.19**	**.24**	**.31**	**.24**	**.19**	**.16**[a]
7. SD Index							1.0	**.14**	**.17**	**.20**	**.50**	**.23**	**.12**	**.31**[a]
8.District								1.0	**.25**	**.16**	-.01	**.63**	.02	.03
9. Mayor									1.0	**.42**	-**.15**	**.80**	**.20**	.05[a]
10. Partisan										1.0	-**.13**	**.72**	**.09**	.02[a]
11. Crime 86											1.0	-**.14**	-**.08**	**.20**[a]
12. TG Index												1.0	**.15**	.05[a]
13. HEW Sp.													1.0	.06[a]
14. AA Mayor														1.0

Note: Correlations in bold p < .10; [a] N=605

Appendix B: Table 2. Correlation Matrix for Chapter 6 Models, N=790.

Variable	1	2	3	4	5	6	7	8	9	10	11	12	13	14
1.Off./ 103 Res.	1.0	.09	.34	-.25	.41	.45	.47	.53	.29	.05	.84	.026	.03	.21^a
2. Ln Pop.91		1.0	.10	.08	.37	.19	.20	.27	.17	-.07	.01	-.02	-.04	.09^a
3. South			1.0	-.01	.36	.01	-.01	.47	.12	-.06	.07	-.13	-.06	.04^a
4. % 5-17				1.0	.05	-.25	-.23	-.02	.28	-.11	.02	-.01	-.04	-.01^a
5. Ln Crime 89					1.0	.15	.32	.45	.39	-.08	.03	-.15	-.09	-.05^a
6. Exp/ Capita						1.0	.46	.20	.10	.08	-.02	.09	.07	.14^a
7. Police $/ Cap							1.0	.20	.01	-.06	-.05	-.11	-.10	-.09^a
8. Ln % Black								1.0	.47	.19	.06	.06	.14	.08^a
9. % Unemp.									1.0	.15	.10	.19	.20	.18^a
10. Partisan										1.0	.17	.42	.72	.19^a
11. District											1.0	.24	.63	.18^a
12. Mayor												1.0	.80	.61^a
13. TG Index													1.0	.48^a
14. Str. Mayor														1.0

Note: Correlations in bold p < .10; ^{a} N=595

Appendix C

OUTLIERS ELIMINATED FROM REPORTED ANALYSES

Studentized residuals are the residual value divided by its standard error. Values larger than 2.0 can be a cause for concern (SAS Institute 1989). The Dffits statistic is a scaled measure of the change in the predicted value of the individual observation based on deleting it from the dataset. The Cook's D statistic is a measure of the change in the overall estimates based on deleting the individual observation. For both Cook's D and Dffits statistics, values greater than 2.0 – can be considered to be potentially influential (Neter et al., 1996). It should be noted, however, that these are rules of thumb rather than firm cutoffs. Therefore, cities that exhibited extreme values on one of the three criteria or values well above the cutoffs listed above on two of the three criteria were excluded from the analyses and are listed below.

Chapter 5
1991: Chicopee, MA; Detroit, MI; Greenville, NC; Huntsville, AL; Las Vegas, NV; Los Angeles, CA; Missoula, MT; North Miami Beach, FL; Pensacola, FL; San Francisco, CA; Washington, DC; Woburn, MA
1981: Gloucester, MA; Hartford, CT; Houston, TX; Las Vegas, NV; Los Angeles, CA; Lowell, MA; Lynn, MA; Norwalk, CT; Revere, MA; Slidell, LA; Waltham, MA; Worcester, MA

Chapter 6
1991: Anchorage, AK; Cupertino, CA; Los Angeles, CA; Washington, DC; Orlando, FL; Indianapolis, IN; Las Vegas, NV; Atlantic City, NJ
1981: Cupertino, CA; Hartford, CT; Washington, DC; Detroit, MI; Las Vegas, NV; Atlantic City, NJ; New York, NY

Index

9 781593 320904